MODERN
Comfort Cooking

FEEL-GOOD FAVORITES MADE FRESH AND NEW

LAUREN GRIER

CREATOR OF
CLIMBING GRIER MOUNTAIN

PAGE STREET
PUBLISHING CO.

PAGE STREET
PUBLISHING CO.

Copyright © 2017 by Lauren Grier

First published in 2017 by

Page Street Publishing Co.

27 Congress Street, Suite 105

Salem, MA 01970

www.pagestreetpublishing.com

Distributed by Macmillan, sales in Canada by The Canadian Manda Group.

21 20 19 18 17   1 2 3 4 5

ISBN-13: 978-1-62414-459-2

ISBN-10: 1-62414-459-4

Library of Congress Control Number: 2017907797

Cover and book design by Page Street Publishing Co.

Photography by Lauren Grier

Printed and bound in China

Dedication

I dedicate this book to my family.

To my husband, Mr. B. My love for you knows no bounds. Thank you for being a stable foundation, who never questioned and always encouraged me to follow my dreams. Thank you for your guidance and reassurance, and thank you for being my soul mate. I love you more than life itself.

To my Mom and Dad, who are my best friends. Without your unconditional love, I would not be the woman I am today. Thank you for always believing in me, being a rock when life felt like too much and letting me be me. I hope I've made you proud.

To my Aunt Joan. You have been an inspiration, in more ways than one. Your discipline and enthusiasm in the kitchen—and in life—are infectious. You helped me to know myself better. It was a pleasure to stand by your side as we made this cookbook come to life.

To John, Sarah, Jordan, Arin, Bryley, Josie and Abe, who are my tribe. I would be lost without each of you, and am thankful that I get to walk on this journey of life with you by my side.

To my grandmother, Mary, who is a beacon of light. Who taught me to be a lady, who taught me to never give up, and most importantly, who taught me that being loved by someone gives you strength, but loving someone gives you courage.

To the Grier family, each and every one of you holds a special place in my heart. Thank you for accepting all my quirks, and supplying motivation to continue on the path of my dreams.

Table Of Contents

Introduction

In 2008, I was living the good life. My husband Mr. B and I lived in downtown Denver, and we loved everything about the Mile High City—our jobs, our friends and our quirky neighborhood. Life was good.

Then, well, 2008 had to go and be . . . 2008. I worked in the financial industry, and that September the bubble burst, the market crashed and, you know what came next. Like many others, I lost my job. I went back and forth from interview to interview, week after week, like a hopeless string of bad blind dates. I won't lie to you: in between, I sulked. Like, hardcore. The thing is . . . it wasn't me. I'm not a born sulker. Maybe that's why, during that sulk-a-thon, I experienced the whole "one door closes and another opens" thing. See, I was clocking heavy hours watching TV, but it was mostly cooking shows (shout out to Ina and Giada!). I was in a slump, but the idea of cooking somehow made me feel a little better. The careful preparation, the rhythm of all the slicing and chopping, the way the pros used all five senses, was mesmerizing. Something started to click.

Now, to that point, my culinary knowledge amounted to a hill of beans—and these beans hadn't even been properly soaked, seasoned or simmered. I could hardly follow package directions, my friends. I had no love for cooking, and in many ways food itself was an afterthought. Like a lot of you, I had childhood memories of fun family dinners, and I remembered times in my life when food had made a sweet moment even sweeter. But I had never felt a true calling, or a passion for putting food at the center of life.

Until, like I said, something clicked. Or snapped, or wiggled, or shimmied or whatever the heck a swordfish does. Because that was the first meal I was inspired to cook. As I watched a Food Network TV host pan-sear a couple of swordfish steaks, I was feeling that click. I got my tookus off the couch and made a grocery list. The TV host was preparing something called Seared Swordfish Steak Sandwiches with Arugula and Lemon Aioli. "WARNING! WARNING! YOU DON'T EVEN KNOW WHAT AN AIOLI IS" went off in my head. I forged ahead anyway.

Returning from the store with a Rosie-the-Riveter "I-can-do-it" attitude, I set to work. I followed my instincts. I poured an obscene amount of olive oil into a pan that was nuclear hot. I even seasoned the frozen swordfish! Then I placed the fish in the smoking oil, and ran screaming out of my smoke-filled apartment as hot oil blasted from the pan. MAY-DAY! MAY-DAY! Things were not clicking. Thankfully, Mr. B happened to come home that very moment. He walked casually to the Stove of Death, moved the pan and turned off the heat. "Next time that happens, which should be never, just move the skillet away from the heat." I had married wisely.

It was uphill from there. I started by nearly burning down my building, and ended up with a newfound crush: food. And cooking. I was bound and determined to improve my culinary skills, so I started cooking at every opportunity, sharpening my skills and reading books like Jacques Pépin's *Complete Techniques* to make my foodie brain bigger. By the time my seventeenth job interview rolled around, I found my priorities

had shifted. I knew my spare cash wouldn't be going toward that pair of cheetah pumps anymore—not when there were pots, pans, graters and onion goggles to be had. I had unlocked my inner chef.

In time, I found that I wanted to put my passion out there. A chance meeting with my friend Jamie back in Kansas made me consider blogging. Eventually I started my blog, Climbing Grier Mountain, on August 5, 2010, with the most awkward post in the history of the Internet. And, just as food had taken over my life, it eventually took over the site. Foodie Fridays became a popular feature, and no surprise there— food blogging as an industry had become a real, official kind of thing. I began to connect with other bloggers and readers, and was thankful I'd chosen such a rewarding path. As I became part of a community, my skills in the kitchen made a big leap, too, and I began to make my own recipes.

Years passed, I tweaked and experimented, failed and succeeded day-by-day. And now you're holding the result.

This cookbook is a testament to failures and successes. I want to share the insights I've gained from countless hours of trials and tribulations in the kitchen. And I want others to know you can teach yourself how to cook, and come out on the other side (mostly) unscathed. Mainly, Modern Comfort Cooking is a cookbook focused on making old favorites feel new again. And fun again. I hope that in reading this book, you come to see food as an important connector in life. It connects us to the past, to ourselves, to the people around us. Comfort food makes the best connections, I think.

And believe me when I say comfort food. I ain't messin' around. Sure, not every recipe here is deep fried or coated in melted chocolate, but what you'll find and make in this book will satisfy both your tummy and soul. These recipes will make you want to sit a little longer at the table, and simply savor the moment. The recipes come from my own connections—they're based on childhood experiences, my travels and everyday life with Mr. B, or what I call "playtime in the kitchen."

I hope this book makes you to WANT to cook, whether you're just starting out, looking to mix things up or simply need a nudge to get back in the kitchen and stir that slow-simmering stew of life. Modern Comfort Cooking can't make you fall in love with cooking, but it can motivate you to cook the kind of food that gives . . . comfort. Which, in the end, isn't that all we really want?

Love and happy cooking,

Lauren Grier

Modern-Day Brunch

Living in Denver, Colorado, Mr. B and I are surrounded by brunch options—full-on fine dining, street fair, on-the-go breakfast burritos or coffee with donuts.

Eventually, we land somewhere that fits our mood and rumbling stomachs. Looking like Margo and Todd from *Christmas Family Vacation*, we order two coffees with cream and sip happily, dressed in our favorite Chuck Taylors and zip-up hoodies. We eat and converse about the latest political shenanigans, what's going on in Denver, our plans for the weekend and sometimes, life goals.

I'm a firm believer that brunch is just as important as dinner when it comes to connecting with others. The recipes in Modern-Day Brunch are my way of showing you that hearty staples like One-Pot Greek Biscuits and Gravy Cobbler (page 29), Hot Fried Chicken and Egg Sandwich (page 10) or Chai-Spiced French Toast Skewers (page 17) deserve a seat at the brunch table. These dishes are meant to be easily assembled, shared among friends and lingered over until the last cup of coffee is finished.

You'll find updated versions of standard staples like Quinoa Cake Huevos Rancheros Eggs Benedict (page 21), Mini Chorizo and Cauliflower Hashbrown Egg Loaves (page 34) and Banh Mi Breakfast Tacos (page 26). Make a few of these recipes on the weekend, and soon you'll have your own modern brunch favorites.

HOT FRIED CHICKEN & EGG SANDWICH

I'm a sucker for juicy, golden fried chicken. Well, who isn't? On the pecking order of comfort food, it's the cock of the walk. And lately, fried chicken has stepped up yet another notch: have you tried hot chicken? Or what some folks call "Nashville hot chicken," because that's where this glorious spicy chicken hails from. This brand of chicken isn't for the faint of heart. In fact, it ought to come with a warning about breathing flames once consumed. In my opinion, it's worth the dragon-level status. The chicken gets its heat from spices like cayenne, paprika and chili powder that are mixed with melted butter and brown sugar, and then mopped onto the meat. Put a piece of hot chicken between two rolls and top with an egg and pickles. That'll get your rooster crowin'!

YIELDS 8 SANDWICHES

4 boneless, skinless chicken thighs, cut in half

2 tsp (4 g) ground paprika

2 tsp (4 g) cayenne pepper

3 tsp (8 g) garlic powder, divided

1 tbsp (9 g) chili powder

1 tsp (2 g) onion powder

2 tsp (6 g) kosher salt, divided

2 tsp (5 g) ground pepper, divided

2 cups (490 ml) buttermilk

9 eggs, divided

2½ cups (300 g) all-purpose flour

Vegetable oil, for frying

1 cup (240 ml) sunflower oil

2 tsp (10 g) brown sugar

8 white rolls

Quick Dill Pickles (page 184), for garnish

Mayonnaise, for garnish

Kitchen Tip: Any leftover fried chicken without the egg can be placed in a paper bag and stored in the fridge. To reheat the chicken, place it on a baking sheet in a 350°F (177°C) oven until warm.

Pat the chicken thighs dry. In a small bowl, combine the paprika, cayenne, 2 teaspoons (4 g) of the garlic powder, chili powder, onion powder, 1 teaspoon of kosher salt and 1 teaspoon of pepper. Reserve 2 tablespoons (18 g) of the spice mixture and set it aside. Meanwhile, cover the chicken thighs with the remaining spice mixture and set them on a large plate, covered, at room temperature for an hour.

Once the chicken has set, whisk together buttermilk and 1 egg in a bowl. In another bowl, combine the flour, 1 teaspoon of kosher salt and 1 teaspoon of black pepper. Take a chicken thigh and dip it into the buttermilk, shaking off any excess. Next, dredge the thigh through the flour and set it on a baking sheet. For a double crunch, dip the thigh in the buttermilk and then dredge through the flour again. Repeat the process until all the chicken thighs have been covered.

Pour the vegetable oil into a large Dutch oven, filling it about 2-inches (5-cm) high. Heat the oil using a fry thermometer to 360°F (182°C). Once the oil is hot, add 3 chicken thighs. You don't want to add all the chicken at once because it will bring the heat down, causing the chicken not to cook properly. Fry the chicken for about 12 minutes, rotating every couple of minutes to keep the chicken from burning.

Once cooked, remove the chicken from the Dutch oven with a pair of tongs and place it on a wire rack to cool slightly. Repeat the process with the remaining chicken.

In a small saucepan, preheat the sunflower oil to medium heat. Add the reserved spices and the brown sugar. Once all the ingredients are combined and heated through, use a pastry brush to brush the spiced oil all over the fried chicken.

Next, preheat a non-stick skillet to medium heat. Crack 4 eggs into the skillet and cook until they are slightly opaque, about 3 to 4 minutes. Remove the eggs and set them aside on a plate. Repeat this process with the remaining 4 eggs.

To assemble the sandwiches, place a chicken thigh on top of a roll bottom. Place the pickles and an egg on top of the fried chicken, followed by a top roll. Repeat until all the chicken sandwiches have been assembled. Garnish with mayonnaise and more pickles.

ALMOND BUTTER & STRAWBERRY CROISSANT PUDDING

Back in grade school, peanut butter and jelly was my jam, y'all! I still crave a PB and J on occasion, but I've decided I need something less prone to disapproving glances. The answer is Almond Butter & Strawberry Croissant Pudding, a grown-up version of your standard peanut butter and jelly. Almond butter mixed with milk, vanilla extract, cinnamon, nutmeg and buttery croissants is topped with fresh strawberries and a little strawberry jam, then baked into a glorious, golden pudding.

SERVES 6

1 cup (250 g) almond butter

2 cups (480 ml) almond milk

6 large eggs

1 cup (200 g) granulated sugar, divided

½ tsp kosher salt

½ tsp ground cinnamon

½ tsp ground nutmeg

2 tsp (10 ml) vanilla extract

8 miniature croissants chopped into 1-inch (2.5-cm) cubes

1 lb (450 g) strawberries, halved

⅔ cup (215 g) strawberry jam, divided

Powdered sugar, for garnish

Preheat the oven to 375°F (191°C). Spray a 13 x 9-inch (33 x 23-cm) baking dish with non-stick cooking spray and set it aside. In a large bowl, add the almond butter. Gently pour the milk into the bowl and whisk the almond butter and milk until they are combined. Next, add the eggs and whisk until incorporated with the almond butter and milk. Add ¾ cup (150 g) of the sugar, the kosher salt, cinnamon, nutmeg and vanilla extract. Stir to combine. Add the croissant cubes to the bowl and toss gently. Next, place a small plate that will fit inside the bowl on top of the cubed croissants. The plate will act as a weight to help the croissant cubes absorb the liquid. Place the bowl into the fridge for at least an hour.

Meanwhile, place the strawberries into a large bowl. Pour ¼ cup (50 g) of granulated sugar over the strawberries and toss to combine. Allow the strawberries to sit at room temperature for about 10 minutes.

Take the prepared baking dish and pour half the croissant mixture into the bottom of the dish. Top with some of the strawberry halves and dollop with ⅓ of a cup (110 g) of the strawberry jam. Repeat this step. Cover the baking dish with foil and bake the pudding for about 1 hour and 15 minutes, checking at around 45 minutes to make sure it's cooking evenly. If the pudding is still obviously wobbly, keep cooking until the sides have pulled away and are golden brown and the center looks cooked. Remove the pudding from the oven and let it rest for about 5 minutes before serving. Garnish with powdered sugar.

Variation: Fancy a peanut butter and grape version? Try using frozen Concord grapes in this pudding. Simply defrost the grapes, strain the juices and add in where strawberries are instructed!

PULLED PORK CHILAQUILES FRITTATA

Give me a plate of chilaquiles and I will be your BFF. I don't know what it is about this tortilla chip-based dish covered in spicy tomato sauce, cheese and topped with a fried egg that makes me all googly-eyed. Usually only Chris Hemsworth has that effect on me. Still, whenever I see chilaquiles on a brunch menu, I'm like an ant to a sugar cube: I MUST have them. Kinda like Chris Hemsworth's biceps. Oops! Did I just say that out loud? Sometimes I can't wait for the weekend to enjoy this traditional Mexican dish, so I take matters into my own hands and make my own version. I slow-cook pulled pork covered in cumin, chili powder, coriander, garlic powder and paprika, and pile it high over crispy tortillas, saucy tomato sauce and cheese. The best part? Instead of a fried egg on top, I mix things up and pour eggs over the entire operation and bake it like a frittata. They're the cheesiest, fluffiest, crispiest chilaquiles you'll ever eat. Make them for Chris Hemsworth and he'll be your new BAE.

SERVES 4

1 tbsp (8 g) chili powder

1 tbsp (8 g) ground paprika

1 tbsp (8 g) ground cumin

1 tbsp (8 g) ground coriander

1 tsp garlic powder

1¼ tsp (9 g) kosher salt, divided

1¼ tsp (4 g) ground pepper, divided

2 lb (900 g) boneless pork shoulder

1½ cups (360 ml) chicken stock

1 (15-oz [425-g]) can fire-roasted tomatoes

2 cups (68 g) yellow corn tortilla chips

2 cups (68 g) blue corn tortilla chips

8 large eggs

⅓ cup (80 ml) whole milk

½ cup (57 g) shredded Monterey jack cheese

½ cup (57 g) shredded mild cheddar cheese

Sour cream, for garnish

Pico de gallo, for garnish

Guacamole, for garnish

Fresh jalapeño rounds, for garnish

In a small bowl, combine the chili powder, paprika, cumin, coriander, garlic powder, 1 teaspoon of kosher salt and 1 teaspoon of ground pepper. Place the boneless pork shoulder into the bottom of a slow cooker. Rub the spices all over the pork. Next, add the chicken stock to the slow cooker. Set the slow cooker to 4 hours on high or 8 hours on low. Once the pork has been cooked, remove it from the slow cooker and shred it with two forks. Set it aside.

Meanwhile, preheat the oven to 375°F (191°C). In an oven-proof skillet, heat the fire-roasted tomatoes over medium heat. Cook for about 3 to 4 minutes to let some of the juice of the tomatoes simmer off. Turn the heat off and begin to layer the tortilla chips into the sauce. Top the tortillas with some of the pulled pork.

In a mixing bowl, whisk together the milk, the eggs, ¼ teaspoon of the kosher salt and ¼ teaspoon of the pepper. Pour the eggs over the pulled pork and tortillas. Top the eggs with the Monterey jack and the cheddar cheese. Place the skillet into the oven and bake for about 25 to 35 minutes or until the eggs have set like a frittata. Remove the skillet from the oven and garnish with sour cream, pico de gallo, guacamole and fresh jalapeño rounds.

Kitchen Tip: Keep the brunch vibes going all week by adding leftover pulled pork to some breakfast tacos!

CHAI-SPICED FRENCH TOAST SKEWERS

I'm on team savory when it comes to brunch. Give me a fried egg with hot sauce and I'm yours for life. But every now and again, I get a random craving for something sweet. Pancakes and waffles are cool, but French toast is extra special, held on permanent reserve for those slow, indulgent Saturday mornings. My version has cubes of thick white bread dredged through a chai-spiced egg batter, cooked until golden brown. Did I mention you have time to skewer these lovely cubes? Yeah. And don't forget to dust with powdered sugar and drizzle with maple syrup. I mean, as if you'd forget to do that!

YIELDS 4 SKEWERS

4 eggs

⅓ cup (80 ml) buttermilk

⅓ cup (80 ml) whole milk

¼ tsp kosher salt

1 tsp vanilla extract

½ cup (119 ml) brewed chai tea

2 tbsp (25 g) granulated sugar

1½ tsp (4 g) ground cinnamon

½ tsp cardamom

¼ tsp ground ginger

¼ tsp ground cloves

¼ tsp ground pepper

8 slices (300 g) Texas Toast, or other thickly-sliced white bread

4 tbsp (60 g) unsalted butter, divided

Powdered sugar, for garnish

Maple syrup, for garnish

In a large bowl whisk together the eggs, buttermilk, whole milk, kosher salt, vanilla extract and chai tea. In another small bowl combine the sugar, cinnamon, cardamom, ginger, cloves and pepper.

Lay the bread slices on a baking sheet. Dust the tops and bottom of each slice with some of the cinnamon sugar mixture. Go as heavy or as light as you want! Next, cut each slice into four 1-inch (2.5-cm) cubes.

Preheat a large skillet to medium heat. Melt 1 tablespoon (14 g) of butter. In batches, lightly dredge the bread cubes through the chai milk mixture making sure to shake off any excess batter. Cook the bread cubes on both sides until golden brown, or for about 4 to 5 minutes. Repeat the process until all the bread cubes have been cooked.

Next, take a skewer and thread on 4 to 5 bread cubes. Place the skewer on a plate. Repeat the process until all the skewers have been assembled. Serve the Chai-Spiced French Toast Skewers with powdered sugar and maple syrup.

Kitchen Tip: Hosting a brunch party? These skewers can be assembled and made ahead of time. To reheat, simply preheat your oven to 375°F (191°C) and line a baking sheet with foil. Spray the foil with non-stick cooking spray and place the skewers on the baking sheet. Place the baking sheet into the oven for about 5 to 7 minutes, or until heated through!

EGG-IN-A-HOLE *with* GREEN GODDESS DRESSING

Whenever we have family or friends coming to town, I make sure to have something in the fridge we can nosh on, especially for breakfast. The ceremony of letting folks wake up casually, sip a hot cup of coffee and talk about plans for the day is something I cherish. My standard company breakfast is an egg casserole that I whip up the night before and slide into the oven the morning of. But time is precious, so I've got a way to feed a crowd even faster! Hold onto your horses, and meet the modern version of an egg casserole: baked egg-in-a-hole. All you have to do is lay bagel slices in a casserole dish, crack an egg into the hole and bake! Breakfast is ready in less than five minutes. But don't forget the green goddess dressing for a little extra nourishment!

SERVES 4 TO 6

3 whole wheat bagels, sliced in half

6 large eggs

2 anchovies packed in oil, drained

1 cup (16 g) packed basil leaves

¼ cup (4 g) packed flat-leaf parsley

1 clove garlic, peeled

¼ cup (4 g) fresh dill

2 tbsp (6 g) chopped jalapeño

½ cup (120 g) Greek yogurt

2 tbsp (30 ml) lemon juice

2 tbsp (30 ml) olive oil

1 tsp salt

½ tsp ground pepper

Avocado slices, for garnish

Cucumber rounds, for garnish

Microgreens, for garnish

Preheat the oven to 400°F (204°C). Spray a 13 x 9-inch (33 x 23-cm) baking dish with non-stick cooking spray. Place bagel slices into the bottom of the baking dish. Depending on your bagel size, you may need to use a small knife to cut a bigger hole to ensure the egg will sit nicely inside the bagel. Crack an egg into each bagel hole. Place the baking dish into the oven and bake the eggs for about 5 minutes, or until the egg whites are set. Remove the baking dish from the oven.

In a food processor blend the anchovies, basil, parsley, garlic, dill, jalapeño, Greek yogurt, lemon juice, olive oil, salt and pepper. Blend until smooth, adjusting the salt and pepper, as needed.

Drizzle the bagels with the green goddess dressing and garnish with avocado, cucumber and microgreens.

Variation: This dish would be fun to serve at a large gathering! Simply make a few batches of baked egg-in-a-hole and provide a toppings bar to go along.

QUINOA CAKE HUEVOS RANCHEROS BENEDICT

Decisions are the worst—especially when it comes to ordering brunch. Two of my go-tos are eggs benedict and huevos rancheros. Both are strong, hearty dishes whose unique flavors make me positively giddy. So, one recent fateful morning, I decided these two should get hitched—and hitched they got! The quinoa cakes in this recipe have the flavors of huevos rancheros stuffed inside. Top the cakes with a poached egg and a spicy hollandaise sauce and you've got a brunch made in heaven.

SERVES 4

QUINOA CAKES

1 tbsp (15 ml) olive oil

½ cup (50 g) chopped shallots

½ cup (90 g) diced green pepper

1½ tsp (9 g) kosher salt, divided

1½ tsp (4 g) ground pepper, divided

4 cups (740 g) cooked quinoa

1 tbsp (8 g) chili powder

1 tsp ground coriander

1 tsp ground cumin

1 tsp ground paprika

1 tsp garlic powder

½ cup (86 g) black beans, drained and rinsed

4 large eggs, whisked

2 cups (100 g) panko

Vegetable oil, for sautéing

Sour cream, for garnish

Pico de gallo, for garnish

Cilantro, for garnish

POACHED EGGS

8 large eggs

HOLLANDAISE SAUCE

1 cup (227 g) unsalted butter

3 egg yolks

2 tbsp (30 ml) lemon juice

½ tsp cayenne pepper

FOR THE QUINOA CAKES

In a skillet preheated to medium-high heat, add the olive oil, shallot, green pepper, ½ teaspoon of kosher salt and ½ teaspoon of ground pepper. Sauté the veggies until softened, about 3 minutes. Remove the skillet from the heat and cool completely.

Once the veggies have cooled, place them in a large bowl. Add the cooked quinoa, chili powder, coriander, cumin, paprika, garlic powder, black beans, eggs, panko, 1 teaspoon of kosher salt and 1 teaspoon of ground pepper. Mix to combine. Take the mixture and form into eight to nine 3½ x 1-inch (9 x 2.5-cm) diameter cakes. You may want to rinse your hands in between forming the cakes. Place the cakes onto a baking sheet, then place them into the fridge to set for at least 1 hour.

Remove the cakes from the fridge. Preheat a large skillet to medium-high heat and add the vegetable oil. Place 4 cakes gently into the skillet and crisp them on both sides, about 2 to 3 minutes each. Remove the crisp cakes from the skillet and place them on a plate. Repeat the process until all the cakes have been cooked.

FOR THE POACHED EGGS

Bring a large pot of water to a boil. Once the water is boiling, with a spoon begin stirring the water in a large, circular motion. A tornado will form, and that's your cue to drop the egg into the water, allowing the egg to stay intact in the whirlpool. Cook the egg for about 2½ minutes and remove it with a slotted spoon. Place the poached egg on top of the quinoa cake. Repeat this process until all the eggs have been poached.

FOR THE HOLLANDAISE SAUCE

In a medium saucepan, melt the butter until it is slightly sizzling. Once the butter has melted, pour the butter into a large liquid measuring cup so you can stream it into the blender. Place the egg yolks into the blender or food processor. Turn the blender on low to allow the yolks to get a running start. Take the warm butter and, while the blender is still on low, gently stream the butter into the blender. Keep pouring the butter until it's gone and then immediately add the lemon juice. If the sauce is too thick, add some more lemon juice and keep blending. Add the cayenne pepper and continue to mix until the sauce is smooth and creamy.

To serve, place 2 quinoa cakes on a plate. Top each cake with a poached egg and hollandaise sauce. Garnish with sour cream, pico de gallo and cilantro.

ULTIMATE AREPAS BREAKFAST BLT

In Colorado, a weekend isn't complete unless you've had brunch. Coloradans take their brunch very seriously, and are constantly on the hunt for the latest and greatest breakfast–lunch tangle. My own recent adventures led me to stumble upon arepas. I discovered these Colombian and Venezuelan white corn cakes stuffed with plantains, pulled pork and a poached egg at a joint nearby, and I instantly fell in love with the simple, bold flavors. The texture from the cornmeal gives this sandwich interpretation a new dimension of flavor, and because you can make it ahead of time, it's a breeze compared to homemade tortillas or bread. I kept this BLT recipe simple to let the arepa flour stand out and keep you coming back for seconds and thirds. Plus, you can't go wrong with a runny egg and bacon in the sandwich mix.

YIELDS 8 SANDWICHES

2 cups (240 g) arepa flour, or precooked cornmeal

2 tsp (12 g) kosher salt

2½ cups (600 ml) warm water

2 tbsp (30 ml) vegetable oil, divided

8 slices of bacon

1 tsp ground pepper

4 large eggs

8 tomato slices

1 cup (75 g) fresh arugula

¼ cup (58 g) mayonnaise

In a large bowl, combine the flour and kosher salt. In the same bowl, make a well in the center and pour in the warm water. Stir the ingredients until they are well incorporated and no longer lumpy. You will want to let the dough rest for about 10 minutes before kneading it in the bowl. Knead the dough for a few minutes, and then divide the dough into 8 pieces. Take each piece of dough and roll it into a ball and then place it on a work surface and flatten it into a ½-inch (1-cm) thick disc.

Add 1 tablespoon (15 ml) of vegetable oil to a skillet preheated to medium heat. Next, add 4 arepas, cover and cook until they become golden brown, or about 5 to 6 minutes. Flip the arepas and cook on the other side, uncovered for about 5 minutes. Transfer to a plate to cool. Add the remaining 1 tablespoon (15 ml) of vegetable oil to the skillet. Add the remaining arepas to the skillet and cook. Transfer to the plate to cool once they are finished cooking.

In another skillet preheated to medium heat, add the bacon and the ground pepper. Cook the bacon until it is crispy, about 7 minutes, flipping it with tongs halfway through. Once it's cooked, remove the bacon and place it on a plate lined with a paper towel.

In the same skillet you used for cooking the bacon, crack 4 large eggs. Cook the eggs for about 2 to 3 minutes, or until the yolk has turned opaque. Next, remove an egg from the skillet and place it on top of an arepa. Top the egg with 2 slices of bacon, ¼ cup (15 g) of arugula and 2 tomato slices. Take another arepa and spread the top with 1 tablespoon (15 ml) of mayonnaise, then place it on top of the sandwich. Repeat the process until all the sandwiches have been assembled!

Kitchen Tip: If arepa flour isn't available at your local supermarket, you can substitute fine-ground cornmeal for it, but make sure it is pre-cooked.

DRAGON FRUIT COCONUT CHIA PUDDING

I've come a long way since the days of eating cold milk and cereal for breakfast, lunch and dinner. Don't get me wrong, I still think poofs, flakes and crunches are excellent options for curing HANGRY-itis. But let's talk about an upgraded version of the morning staple: meet chia pudding, a lovely option for breakfast or dessert. Two glorious things about chia pudding are it's good for you because chia seeds are an ancient superfood bursting with antioxidants, and there's no fuss. Everything is mixed into a bowl and placed in the fridge to soak overnight. All you have to do is pull the cold pudding out the next morning and add toppings like dragon fruit smoothie mix, quinoa and crispy maple granola! Your HANGRY-self will totally approve.

SERVES 4

COCONUT CRISP TOPPING

½ cup (15 g) rice crisp cereal

¼ cup (26 g) plain granola

1½ tbsp (12 g) unsweetened coconut flakes

1 tbsp (15 ml) agave syrup

CHIA PUDDING

2 cups (480 ml) coconut-flavored almond milk

6 tbsp (10 g) chia seeds

2 tbsp (15 ml) agave syrup

1 tsp vanilla extract

¼ tsp kosher salt

1 cup (185 g) cooked black quinoa

1 frozen dragon fruit smoothie pack, such as Pitaya Plus, slightly thawed by running under cold water

½ cup (120 ml) coconut water

1 banana, sliced

FOR THE COCONUT CRISP TOPPING

In a large bowl, mix the rice crisps, plain granola, coconut flakes and agave syrup. Store the topping in the fridge until it's needed.

FOR THE CHIA PUDDING

In a large bowl, combine the almond milk, chia seeds, agave syrup, vanilla extract and kosher salt. Cover and place in the fridge for at least 4 hours or up to 24 hours, for better results. Remove the chia pudding from the fridge and stir. Divide the pudding among four to five wide-rimmed glasses. Next, spoon a layer of quinoa into each glass filled with the chia pudding. In a small food processor or blender, add the dragon fruit smoothie pack, coconut water and banana. Pulse until smooth. Pour the dragon fruit mix over the quinoa, and top with the coconut crisp topping. Repeat the process until all the glasses have been assembled.

Variation: Don't have almond milk in the fridge? Simply use whatever you have on hand—whole milk, skim milk or soy milk!

BANH MI BREAKFAST TACOS

Every Friday morning I make Mr. B a breakfast taco. It's "our" reward for finishing a crazy week, and gets us excited for the weekend ahead. Typically, I serve up my breakfast tacos with chorizo as the star, but lately these Banh Mi Breakfast Tacos have been in heavy rotation. The key to these beauties is the pickled carrots and daikon—with a little prep ahead of time, they add the perfect crunch. Drizzle a little Sriracha aioli on top and you'll be ready for the weekend in 3, 2, 1 . . .

YIELDS 8 TACOS

1 cup (240 ml) water

¼ cup (56 g) granulated sugar

¼ cup (59 ml) white vinegar

¼ cup (59 ml) rice wine vinegar

1 tbsp (17 g) plus ¼ tsp kosher salt, divided

3 small, peeled carrots

1 large, peeled daikon

6 slices bacon

6 large eggs

1 tbsp (15 ml) half-and-half

¼ cup (28 g) shredded mild cheddar cheese

¾ cup (174 g) mayonnaise

1 tbsp (15 ml) Sriracha

1 tbsp (15 ml) lemon juice

¼ tsp ground pepper

8 taco-size soft flour tortillas, toasted

Seedless cucumber sliced into rounds, for garnish

Jalapeño rounds, for garnish

Fresh cilantro, for garnish

To make the pickled carrots and daikon, in a large bowl combine the water, granulated sugar, white vinegar, rice wine vinegar and 1 tablespoon (17 g) of the kosher salt. Next, chop the carrots and daikon into ¼-inch (0.6-cm) thick matchsticks. Place the carrots and daikon into the vinegar mixture and let them sit for at least 30 minutes.

Preheat the oven to 400°F (204°C). Line a baking sheet with foil and spray with non-stick cooking spray. Place the bacon on top of the foil and bake it for about 12 to 15 minutes, or until crispy. Remove the bacon from the oven, and transfer to a plate lined with a paper towel. Once cooled, roughly chop the bacon.

Meanwhile, crack the eggs into a bowl. Add the half-and-half, cheese and cooked bacon, and whisk until combined. Preheat a non-stick skillet to medium heat and add the egg mixture. Cook the eggs until they're scrambled and fluffy, about 5 minutes. Remove the skillet from the heat.

In a small bowl, combine the mayonnaise, Sriracha, lemon juice, remaining ¼ teaspoon of kosher salt and ¼ teaspoon of ground pepper. Set this mixture aside.

To assemble the tacos, take a tortilla and add some of the scrambled eggs. Top the eggs with a few carrot and daikon matchsticks, followed by cucumber slices, jalapeños and fresh cilantro. Drizzle the top with Sriracha aioli. Repeat the process with the remaining tacos.

Kitchen Tip: Make the pickled carrots and daikon ahead of time. Keep in the fridge in an airtight container for up to a week.

ONE-POT GREEK BISCUITS & GRAVY COBBLER

Order-envy-itis. Ever experience this? It's when you go against your better judgment and order the wrong dish, even though you were craving those biscuits and gravy. Now you have to sit and watch your friend, who's devouring a plate of breakfast heaven while you choke down an over-cooked omelet. Please—don't let order-envy-itis ruin your Sunday morning! Take control, take your morning back and make your own biscuits and gravy! You can start with this One-Pot Greek Biscuits and Gravy Cobbler. All the staples of good ol' fashioned biscuits and gravy like grandma used to cook, but with Greek flare. Oregano gravy topped with buttery biscuits, feta, tomatoes and olives. Bonus: you don't need to share this one-pot dish with anybody. Okay, maybe give yia-yia a bite.

SERVES 4

1 tbsp (15 ml) olive oil

1 lb (450 g) ground breakfast pork or lamb sausage

¼ cup (36 g) all-purpose flour

2 tsp (5 g) ground oregano, divided

1 tsp garlic powder

1 tsp ground cumin

¼ tsp kosher salt

¼ tsp ground pepper

3 cups (700 ml) whole milk

1 (16-oz [450-g]) can prepared biscuits

3 tbsp (42 g) unsalted butter, melted

Grape tomatoes, for garnish

Kalamata olives, for garnish

Crumbled feta, for garnish

Fresh mint, for garnish

Preheat the oven to 350°F (177°C).

In a large 10-inch (25-cm) cast-iron skillet preheated to medium heat, add the olive oil and the sausage. Cook the sausage, breaking it up with a wooden spoon, until it is no longer pink, about 5 minutes. Once it's cooked, strain the sausage with a slotted spoon, removing any excess fat from the skillet. Then, add the cooked sausage back to the skillet. Next, add the flour, 1½ teaspoons (4 g) of the oregano, garlic powder, cumin, kosher salt and ground pepper. Stir to combine, making sure everything is well mixed. Pour the milk into the skillet and continue to stir for about 5 minutes, until the gravy has thickened.

Remove the skillet from the heat, and top the gravy with the biscuits. Mix the melted butter with the remaining ½ teaspoon of oregano. Brush the tops of the biscuits with the oregano butter, and place the skillet into the oven for about 10 to 15 minutes, or until the biscuits are cooked through. Remove the skillet from the oven and garnish with the grape tomatoes, kalamata olives, feta and mint.

Kitchen Tip: Save some time and make the biscuits a day ahead! Store the biscuits in an airtight container and remove them when you need to top the gravy!

SAVORY TUSCAN FARRO BREAKFAST BOWLS

Is it me, or do most breakfast-eaters tend to favor sweet over savory? I feel outnumbered when there's a breakfast gathering and someone heroically waltzes in with a box of donuts. Don't get me wrong, I love donuts. I just can't start my day off eating one, because the likelihood of me tackling someone from the sugar rush is surprisingly high. Well, here's one great reason to give sugar a little rest: Savory Tuscan Farro Breakfast Bowls. The beauty of this recipe is that no bowl is the same! Can I get a high-five? Fluffy farro is topped with roasted tomatoes, pesto, a soft-boiled egg, chickpeas, roasted red peppers, avocado, Greek yogurt and a good dusting of freshly grated Parmesan. You'll feel like you're savoring the Tuscan sun.

SERVES 4

3 cups (447 g) halved grape tomatoes

2 tbsp (30 ml) olive oil

1 tsp kosher salt

1 tsp ground pepper

2 cups (480 ml) water

1 cup (185 g) dried farro

¼ cup (56 g) basil pesto

4 soft-boiled eggs, peeled

1 cup (152 g) chickpeas, drained and rinsed

4 roasted red peppers, sliced thinly

1 avocado, sliced thinly

Freshly grated Parmesan, for garnish

Preheat the oven to 400°F (204°C). Spray a 9 x 9-inch (23 x 23-cm) baking dish with non-stick cooking spray. Add the tomatoes to the prepared baking dish. Toss with the olive oil, kosher salt and ground pepper. Roast the tomatoes for about 20 minutes, or until golden brown and slightly shriveled. Remove the tomatoes from the oven, and set them aside to cool.

In a large pot, add the water and farro. Bring the water to a boil, and cook the farro according to the package instructions. Once the farro has absorbed all the water, remove the pot from the heat and set it aside.

To assemble, divide the farro among four bowls. Top each bowl with the roasted tomatoes, 1 tablespoon (14 g) of pesto, 1 sliced egg, ¼ cup (38 g) of the chickpeas, 1 roasted red pepper, avocado slices and Parmesan!

Kitchen Tip: Save yourself a little time in the morning by making the farro a few days ahead. Keep it in the fridge until you're ready to use it! Or if you don't have farro on hand, brown rice or quinoa works great, too!

PUMPKIN SNICKERDOODLE DUTCH BABY

When it comes to making brunch at home on the weekends, I'm all about the path of least resistance. If I haven't been compromised the night before, sure, I might be flipping pancakes or busting out the waffle iron. But nine times out of ten, I want everything ready to go in one bowl. Enter the Pumpkin Snickerdoodle Dutch Baby. All the ingredients are mixed into a single bowl, then poured into a cast-iron skillet and baked to golden perfection. This version tastes like a giant snickerdoodle cookie, with a warm kick from the cinnamon pumpkin mixture. Drizzle the top with maple syrup and a dollop of whipped cream, and go get your weekend on!

SERVES 4

2 tbsp (25 g) granulated sugar

1 tsp ground cinnamon

3 large eggs

½ cup (120 ml) whole milk

½ cup (60 g) all-purpose flour

¼ cup (55 g) pumpkin puree

1 tsp vanilla extract

¼ tsp kosher salt

½ tsp pumpkin spice

1 tbsp (14 g) unsalted butter

Whipped cream, for garnish

Maple syrup, for garnish

Powdered sugar, for garnish

Vanilla ice cream, for garnish

Preheat the oven to 450°F (232°C). Place a 10-inch (25-cm) cast-iron skillet into the oven until the Dutch baby is ready to assemble.

To make the cinnamon sugar mix, in a small bowl combine the granulated sugar and the cinnamon. Set the bowl aside.

To make the pancake batter, in a large mixing bowl whisk the eggs. Pour the milk into the bowl and continue to whisk. Add in the flour, pumpkin puree, vanilla extract, kosher salt and pumpkin spice. Mix all the ingredients until everything is well combined.

Making sure to use an oven mitt, remove the hot skillet from the oven, and immediately add the butter. Once the butter has coated the bottom of the skillet, add the pancake batter. Sprinkle the cinnamon sugar mixture on top of the pancake. Place the skillet back in the oven and bake the pancake until it is puffed and golden brown, about 20 to 25 minutes. Remove from the oven and garnish with whipped cream, maple syrup, powdered sugar and vanilla ice cream!

Kitchen Tip: The batter can be prepared ahead of time. Simply mix all the ingredients in a bowl, cover and place the bowl in the fridge until it is ready to use!

MINI CHORIZO & CAULIFLOWER HASHBROWN EGG LOAVES

On weekday mornings, the struggle is real. And the last thing I want to think about is making breakfast. We've all been there. If I need to do ONE. MORE. THING. to get out the door, I might just lose it! Okay, so maybe it's not quite that bad. But these Mini Chorizo and Cauliflower Hashbrown Egg Loaves are a reminder of an underrated strategy: the make-ahead. Prebake the cauliflower mixture the night before, and top with cooked chorizo. The morning of, crack an egg into the loaf tin and BOOM! A hot, cheesy, sassy meal in 10 minutes or less.

SERVES 4 TO 5

2 (1-lb [450-g]) heads of cauliflower

1 tsp kosher salt, plus a pinch

12 large eggs, divided

1 tsp ground cumin

1 tsp garlic powder

1½ cups (150 g) shredded mozzarella cheese, plus more for garnish

1 cup (100 g) shredded mild cheddar cheese

1 tsp ground pepper

1 tbsp (15 ml) olive oil

½ lb (230 g) freshly ground pork chorizo

Cotija cheese, for garnish

Fresh cilantro, for garnish

Pico de gallo, for garnish

Fresh jalapeño rounds, for garnish

Kitchen Tip: Don't have a mini loaf pan handy? This recipe works great in a muffin tin, too!

Variation: Want to mix things up? Add in any protein you'd prefer, like breakfast pork sausage, bacon or leftovers from the night before!

Preheat the oven to 375°F (191°C). Using a knife, cut each cauliflower head into florets. Next, bring a large pot of water to a boil, and add a pinch of salt. Add the cauliflower florets to the boiling water and cook until the florets are slightly tender, or about 5 minutes. Remove the cauliflower from the pot with a slotted spoon and place the florets in a large food processor.

Pulse the florets until they resemble a finely crumbled grain. Once the cauliflower has been processed, let it cool slightly before placing it on a large kitchen towel. This way you won't burn your hands when you squeeze out the excess water! Grab the towel ends and cover the cauliflower. Wring the cauliflower by squeezing the water into a bowl. You might have to repeat this process a few times, until most of the liquid has been removed and the cauliflower is dry.

Next, place the cauliflower into a large bowl. Add 2 large eggs, the cumin, garlic powder, 1½ cups (150 g) of the mozzarella, the cheddar cheese, 1 teaspoon of kosher salt and the pepper. Gently mix the cauliflower until all the ingredients are incorporated. Spray 5 mini loaf tins with non-stick cooking spray. Divide the cauliflower mixture, using about ¾ cup (245 g) per mini loaf tin. With your fingers, pat the cauliflower mixture down so it forms an even layer. Place the mini loaf tins on a baking sheet and bake them for about 15 minutes, or until they are firm.

Meanwhile, preheat a skillet to medium-high heat. Add the olive oil and chorizo to the skillet. Cook the chorizo, breaking it up with a wooden spoon. Cook it until it is no longer pink, or about 6 minutes. Remove the chorizo from the skillet using a slotted spoon, and place it in a bowl and set aside.

Once the cauliflower is done baking, remove the muffin loaves from the oven. Take some of the chorizo and sprinkle it on top of the cauliflower. Next, crack 2 eggs, being careful not to break the yolks, and place them on top of the chorizo. Sprinkle 1 tablespoon (3 g) of mozzarella over the eggs. Repeat the process with the remaining cauliflower loaves. Place the loaves back into the oven and bake them for about 10 minutes, or until the egg is slightly opaque.

Feel free to serve the loaves in the loaf pans, or unmold them onto a pretty plate. Garnish the tops with Cojita cheese, cilantro, pico de gallo and fresh jalapeño rounds.

East Meets West

I was bitten by the travel bug late in life. For the longest time, I was happy to be a homebody. My days were simple and predictable. Yes, I was that homesick little girl who called her parents to come pick her up in the middle of a sleepover. Honestly, I'm not sure how I got through college.

Years later, that quiet, homebody girl grew up. It was a trip to London during one college spring break that awakened a desire to broaden my horizons. After that trip, I decided to put on my big-girl travel undies and face my fear of the unknown. I wanted to see the world. Now I feel lucky to have a career that has sent me around the United States, Europe, Central America and, my most recent favorite, the Far East.

There is nothing like touching down in a country that is completely foreign. The smells, the terrain, the people; your senses are thrown out of whack and your world is turned upside-down, all in the very best way. I hope you'll find dishes in this chapter that expand your palate. I've taken spices and sauces from places like Japan, the Middle East, Korea and India, and plugged them neatly into western dishes. From Indian Spiced Fried Chicken (page 42), to Thai Chicken and Dumplings (page 45) to Asian-Style Sloppy Joes (page 57), I hope these dishes make you think about home in whole new way.

KOREAN BBQ BURGER *with* MISO-CANDIED BACON

If you've been on the lookout for a decadent, international comfort-food burger, this Korean BBQ Burger with Miso-Candied Bacon is it! To think of all the flavors this burger is bursting with is, simply, to drool. Fresh ginger, soy sauce, scallions, sesame oil and gochugjang all bring it strong. By the way, if you don't know what gochugjang is, run to the grocery store and pick yourself up a bottle. It's a Korean barbeque sauce that's a perfect blend of spicy, sweet and savory. Smother it on top of a burger with cheddar cheese and dangerously easy miso-candied bacon. Better make seconds, thirds and fifths.

SERVES 4

MISO-CANDIED BACON

½ lb (220 g) bacon, or about 10 slices

½ cup (138 g) white miso paste

¼ cup (60 ml) maple syrup

1 cup (237 ml) rice wine vinegar

¾ cup (177 ml) mirin

KOREAN BBQ BURGER

1½ lb (681 g) lean ground beef

1½ tbsp (23 g) freshly grated, peeled ginger

¼ cup (25 g) chopped scallions

2 cloves garlic, minced

1 tbsp (15 ml) sesame oil

3 tbsp (45 ml) soy sauce

¼ tsp kosher salt

¼ tsp ground pepper

3 tbsp (42 g) clarified butter (page 183)

¼ cup (237 ml) gochugjang (Korean barbecue sauce)

4 slices mild cheddar cheese

4 brioche buns, toasted

Lettuce, for garnish

Tomato slices, for garnish

FOR THE MISO-CANDIED BACON

Preheat the oven to 375°F (191°C).

Line a baking sheet with foil and spray with it with non-stick cooking spray. Place 10 slices of bacon on top of the foil. Place the bacon into the oven and bake it for about 7 minutes, then flip over the bacon and cook it on the other side for an additional 3 minutes. Remove the baking sheet from the oven.

Meanwhile, in a saucepan preheated to medium heat, add the miso paste, maple syrup, rice wine vinegar and mirin. Stir to combine. Reduce the temperature to a simmer and let the sauce reduce until thickened, or about 15 minutes.

Brush the miso glaze on top of the bacon and return the bacon back to the oven for about 2 to 3 minutes, or until it gets crispy. Remove the bacon from the oven and place the bacon on the plate lined with a paper towel.

FOR THE KOREAN BBQ BURGER

In a large bowl combine the ground beef, ginger, scallions, garlic, sesame oil, soy sauce, kosher salt and ground pepper. Take the mixture and form it into four 6-ounce (170-g) patties, about 1-inch (2.5-cm) thick. Preheat a cast-iron skillet to medium-high heat and add the clarified butter. Place the burgers in the skillet and cook them for about 3 to 4 minutes. Flip, and glaze each burger with 1 teaspoon of the gochugjang. Continue to cook the burgers for another 3 minutes, and in the last minute of cooking, place a slice of cheese on top. Let the cheese melt and remove the burgers to a plate to rest for at least 5 minutes. Take a toasted brioche bun and place a patty on the bottom bun. Top with lettuce, tomato, miso-candied bacon, followed by the remaining top bun. Repeat the process until all the burgers have been assembled.

Kitchen Tip: Once you've formed your burgers, if you have time, place them into the fridge for at least an hour, or up to 24 hours, to let the flavors set. Remove them from the fridge and go straight to the hot skillet.

MOROCCAN MEATLOAF *with* TOMATO-HARISSA SAUCE

"MA! MEATLOAF!" Or at least that's what my inner child monologue would say when I was craving comfort food. Meatloaf is actually one of the top favorite foods among Americans, but it's also widely popular in other countries. For my take, I imagined what this dish might look like if conjured up in a Moroccan kitchen. There's ground lamb, mixed with cinnamon, ginger, turmeric, paprika, cumin and cayenne. Once you've combined the loaf, place it in the oven, and the aroma will have you feeling like you're walking through a Moroccan spice shop. It's topped off with a delicious tomato-harrisa sauce. All right, folks, let's get meatloaf trending again!

SERVES 4

1½ lb (681 g) ground lamb

1 tsp ground cinnamon

1 tsp ground ginger

1 tsp ground turmeric

1 tsp ground paprika

1 tsp ground cumin

¼ tsp cayenne

1 large egg

½ cup (75 g) diced yellow onion

1 cup (237 ml) whole milk

1 cup (50 g) panko

½ tsp kosher salt

½ tsp ground pepper

1 (6-oz [170-g]) can tomato sauce

2 tbsp (27 g) brown sugar

2 tbsp (30 g) prepared harissa

Preheat the oven to 350°F (177°C).

In a large bowl, combine the lamb, cinnamon, ginger, turmeric, paprika, cumin, cayenne, egg, onion, milk, panko, kosher salt and ground pepper. Gently press the lamb mixture into a 5 x 9-inch (13 x 23-cm) loaf pan that has been sprayed with non-stick cooking spray. Bake the meatloaf for about 25 minutes. Remove the meatloaf from the oven and strain off any excess fat or juices that have accumulated.

Meanwhile, in a medium bowl, combine the tomato sauce, brown sugar and harissa. Pour the tomato-harissa sauce over the top of the meatloaf. Place the meatloaf back into the oven and continue to bake it for additional 25 minutes, or until it reaches an internal temperature of 150°F (66°C). Remove the meatloaf from oven and let it rest for 20 minutes before slicing.

Variation: Hungry and don't want to wait a full hour? Spoon the meatloaf mixture into 12 muffin cups to make mini meatloaves. Bake the mini meatloaves for 20 to 25 minutes at 400°F (204°C), adding the sauce halfway through the baking, and you'll have dinner in no time!

INDIAN SPICED FRIED CHICKEN DRUMSTICKS *with* GINGER HONEY

Fried chicken holds a special place in my heart. Whenever I'm craving comfort food, a big plate of breaded bird is my go-to. I like it Nashville-hot, buttermilk-dipped, garlicky or Southern fried. As a fried chicken enthusiast, I'm always looking for new ways to flavor-up this classic comfort dish. For this take, I went all the way around the world and found that Indian spices—garam masala, turmeric and cardamom—make some seriously good fried chicken. The key here is rubbing the chicken with the spices and allowing it to sit at room temperature for one hour. It may seem like a long time, but I'm telling you—after you sink your teeth into that first bite of that juicy, fried drumstick—you'll know it was worth the wait.

YIELDS 8 DRUMSTICKS

1 tsp (2 g) freshly grated ginger

⅓ cup (79 ml) honey

2 tsp (5 g) garam masala

2 tsp (5 g) ground cumin

2 tsp (5 g) ground turmeric

½ tsp ground coriander

¾ tsp cayenne

¾ tsp cardamom

2 tsp (12 g) kosher salt, divided

2 tsp (7 g) ground pepper, divided

3 lb (1.4 kg) chicken drumsticks, or about 8 drumsticks

2 cups (474 ml) buttermilk

1 large egg, whisked

2½ cups (300 g) all-purpose flour

Vegetable oil, for frying

In a bowl, whisk together the ginger and the honey. Set the mixture aside.

Wash the drumsticks and pat them dry. In a bowl, combine the garam masala, cumin, turmeric, coriander, cayenne, cardamom, 1 teaspoon of the kosher salt and 1 teaspoon of ground pepper. Coat the chicken with the spices and set it on a large plate, covered, at room temperature for an hour.

In a bowl, whisk together the buttermilk and the egg. In another bowl, combine the flour, 1 teaspoon of kosher salt and 1 teaspoon of black pepper. Take a drumstick and dip it into the buttermilk, shaking off any excess. Next, dredge the drumstick through the flour and set it on a baking sheet equipped with a wire rack. Repeat the process until all the drumsticks have been covered.

In a large Dutch oven, pour in the vegetable oil with enough oil to cover three-quarters of the drumsticks. Heat the Dutch oven to medium-high heat. You'll know when the oil is hot when you sprinkle some flour into the oil and it starts to sizzle. Once the oil is hot, add 3 drumsticks. You don't want to add all the drumsticks at once because it will bring the heat down, causing the chicken to not cook properly. Fry the drumsticks for about 12 to 16 minutes, rotating every couple of minutes to keep the chicken from burning.

Check that the chicken is cooked to 165°F (74°C) by inserting an instant-read thermometer into the drumstick, being careful not to touch the bone. Then remove the drumsticks and place them on a wire rack to cool slightly. Repeat the process with the remaining drumsticks, adding more oil to the Dutch oven, as needed. Drizzle the drumsticks with the ginger honey as a final step.

Kitchen Tip: If you don't have a candy thermometer, use an instant-read thermometer to test the oil temperature from time-to-time. Keeping the temperature between 350° and 360°F (177° and 182°C) will help achieve a golden crust and let the chicken be completely cooked through.

THAI CHICKEN & DUMPLINGS

I have fond childhood memories of my mom making chicken and dumplings. The weather was bone-chilling cold whenever this weeknight meal would make an appearance. To keep us entertained, my mother would let us help in the kitchen—not so much with the searing of the chicken, but with the pouring and whisking of the dumplings. I remember standing on a stool and reaching over to spoon the dumpling mixture on top of the chicken. Then mom would cover the pot for what seemed like an eternity, which was actually only ten minutes, and we'd watch in wonder as the dish was unveiled. The pancake-like batter had transformed into fluffy, little flavor-clouds. It was magical! Sure enough, my Thai version of that classic dish is full of its own kind of magic. The foundation is still the same, with a little kick from fresh ginger, red curry paste and coconut milk. Add in coriander dumplings, and this is a soup that warms the soul!

SERVES 4

DUMPLINGS

1 cup (140 g) all-purpose flour

2 tsp (5 g) baking powder

1 tsp ground coriander

½ tsp kosher salt

½ tsp ground pepper

⅝ cup (148 ml) whole milk, divided

THAI CHICKEN

2 tbsp (30 g) red curry paste

2 tbsp (30 ml) red chili sauce

2 cloves garlic, minced

2 tbsp (12 g) minced fresh ginger

4 to 5 bone-in, skin-on chicken thighs

1½ tsp (9 g) kosher salt, divided

1½ tsp (4 g) ground pepper, divided

3 tbsp (43 g) clarified butter (page 183)

2 cups (256 g) diced carrots

1 cup (150 g) diced yellow onion

1 tbsp (15 ml) white wine

1 (14-oz [397-g]) can unsweetened coconut milk, gently stirred

1 cup (237 ml) chicken stock

1½ cups (225 g) frozen or fresh peas

FOR THE DUMPLINGS

In a medium bowl, combine the flour, baking powder, coriander, kosher salt and ground pepper. Gradually add 8 tablespoons (120 ml) of milk, whisking to make the batter light and fluffy. Add 2 tablespoons (30 ml) of milk if the batter is too thick.

FOR THE THAI CHICKEN

In a medium bowl, combine the curry paste, chili sauce, garlic and ginger. Set the mixture aside. Place the chicken thighs on a plate and sprinkle each side with ½ teaspoon of kosher salt and ½ teaspoon of ground pepper. Next, preheat a large Dutch oven to medium-high heat. Add the clarified butter. Remove any excess fat from the chicken and place the chicken skin-side down and brown it for about 3 minutes. Then, flip, and brown the other side for another 2 minutes. Remove the chicken from the Dutch oven and set it on a plate. Remove all but 2 tablespoons (30 g) of oil from the Dutch oven. In the same Dutch oven, add the carrots. Sauté the carrots for about 4 minutes, or until slightly softened. Next, add the onions along with ¼ teaspoon of kosher salt and ¼ teaspoon of ground pepper. Stir to combine, and cook for another 3 minutes. Add the ginger mixture, followed by the white wine, making sure to scrape up the brown bits from the bottom of the Dutch oven. Pour in the coconut milk and chicken stock. Bring to a simmer and then add the chicken thighs back to the Dutch oven. Simmer covered for about 15 minutes. Add the peas and simmer for an additional 5 minutes.

Once the chicken is done cooking, take about 2 to 3 tablespoons (30 to 44 ml) of the dumpling mixture and spoon it on top of each of the chicken thighs. You'll want to turn the heat to a low simmer and cover the Dutch oven with a lid. Steam the dumplings for about 10 to 15 minutes. Check the dumplings after about 10 minutes to make sure the batter is fully cooked and fluffy. If the batter is still soggy, place the lid back on and continue to cook. Once cooked, the dumplings should be light and fluffy.

Kitchen Tip: To keep things on the healthier side, remove the skins from the chicken thighs!

KOREAN PULLED PORK LASAGNA

The art of slow cooking a piece of meat is something to celebrate. It takes an abundance of patience, preparation and, as the aromas start to fill every room of the house, restraint. If you think you've got the willpower to "set it and forget it," this Korean Pulled Pork Lasagna packs the ultimate payoff. Boneless pork roast is covered in a Korean barbecue sauce, cooked low and slow, then layered between ricotta, veggies and noodles. It's the ultimate comfort food!

SERVES 4 TO 6

2½ lb (1.14 kg) boneless pork roast

1½ cups (350 ml) gochujang (Korean barbecue sauce), divided

1½ cups (350 ml) beef broth

1 tbsp (15 ml) olive oil

1½ cups (165 g) chopped baby bella mushrooms

1 cup (210 g) diced yellow onion

1½ tsp (9 g) kosher salt, divided

1½ tsp (4 g) ground pepper, divided

2 cups (250 g) whole milk ricotta

1 large egg

2 cups (226 g) shredded mild cheddar cheese

2 cups (226 g) shredded mozzarella cheese

12 no-boil, oven-ready lasagna noodles

In a slow cooker, combine the pork roast, ½ cup (119 ml) of the gochujang and the beef broth. Set the slow cooker to high for 4 hours or low for 8 hours. Once cooked, keep the pork in the slow cooker and shred it using two forks. Leave the pork in the juices until it is ready to assemble so it stays nice and juicy!

Preheat the oven to 400°F (204°C). In a large skillet, heat the olive oil over medium-high heat. Sauté the mushrooms for about 3 to 4 minutes, or until lightly browned. Next, add the onions, 1 teaspoon of the salt and 1 teaspoon of pepper. Continue to sauté the veggies for about 5 minutes or until they are softened, adding more olive oil if needed. Turn off the heat and set the skillet aside.

In a large bowl, combine the whole milk ricotta, the egg, ½ teaspoon of kosher salt and ½ teaspoon of ground pepper.

Spray a 13 x 9-inch (33 x 23-cm) baking dish with non-stick cooking spray. Pour ¼ cup (59 ml) of the gochujang sauce and ¼ cup (59 ml) of the pork broth from the slow cooker over the bottom of the dish. Use the back of the spoon to spread the sauce. Take 3 noodles and place them over the sauce. Next, remove some of the pulled pork and ¼ cup (59 ml) of the broth from the slow cooker and place it on top of the noodles in an even layer. Spread some of the veggie mixture over the top of the pulled pork, followed by dollops of the ricotta and ½ cup (57 g) of the cheddar cheese and the mozzarella. Repeat these steps two more times. Top the final noodle with ¼ cup (59 ml) gochujang sauce, spreading it with the bottom of a spoon, 2 tablespoons (30 ml) of the pork broth and the remaining cheese. Cover the baking dish with foil and bake the lasagna for about 45 minutes. Remove the foil and bake for another 10 minutes, or until the cheese is bubbling. Once the lasagna is done baking, remove it from oven and let it set for about 10 minutes before serving!

Kitchen Tip: Lasagna is a great dish to prep for someone who needs a little comfort! Assemble the dish for them and whenever they need a bite of cheesy, delicious lasagna, simply have them slide it into the oven to reheat for a fabulous meal.

INDIAN CHICKEN POT PIE

Spring break, London, England. It's ten years ago, and I'm visiting my uncles across the pond. It's 5 a.m., and after a long night of shenanigans, something very important is about to happen: I'm about to eat Indian food for the first time. It happens slowly at first, but soon I'm devouring dosa, tandoori chicken and some kind of curry, like it's my job. From that moment on, I'm an Indian enthusiast, and that's how this Indian Pot Pie came to be. Toss garam masala, turmeric, cumin, cinnamon and paprika with some chicken thighs and your standard pot pie filling, and don't forget the puff pastry. This pot pie is your ticket to India, sans the jet lag.

SERVES 4

1½ lb (680 g) boneless, skinless chicken thighs, cubed

1½ tbsp (5 g) garam masala

1½ tbsp (5 g) ground cumin

1 tbsp (3 g) ground turmeric

1 tsp ground ground paprika

½ tsp ground cinnamon

1½ tsp (9 g) kosher salt, divided

1½ tsp (4 g) ground pepper, divided

2 tbsp (28 g) clarified butter (page 183)

1 tbsp (15 ml) olive oil

1 cup (111 g) peeled and chopped carrots

1 cup (102 g) chopped celery

1 cup (150 g) chopped yellow onion

2 cloves garlic, minced

1 tbsp (10 g) freshly grated ginger

2 tbsp (18 g) all-purpose flour

⅔ cup (160 ml) whole milk

1½ cups (360 ml) chicken stock

1 cup (153 g) frozen peas

1 sheet frozen puff pastry, thawed

1 large egg

In a large bowl combine the chicken thighs, garam masala, cumin, turmeric, paprika, cinnamon, 1 teaspoon of kosher salt and 1 teaspoon of ground pepper. Stir to combine, making sure all the ingredients are mixed well. Cover the bowl with a towel and let the chicken sit out on the counter for an hour at room temperature to let the flavors set.

Once an hour has passed, preheat a large Dutch oven to medium heat, add the clarified butter and the chicken thighs and sauté the thighs until they are browned and cooked through, about 5 minutes. Remove the chicken thighs from the Dutch oven with tongs, place them on a plate and set them aside.

In the same Dutch oven where you browned the chicken, add the olive oil then add the carrots, celery, onion, garlic, ginger, ½ teaspoon of kosher salt and ½ teaspoon of the ground pepper. Sauté the veggies until they are softened, or about 5 minutes. Next, add the flour and begin to whisk, letting the flour cook out for about 1 minute. Gradually pour in the milk and the chicken stock. Continue to stir. Add the cooked chicken thighs back to the Dutch oven. Bring the sauce to a boil and then to a simmer. Simmer it for about 15 minutes, or until it is slightly thickened. You'll want to check the chicken every 5 minutes or so to make sure it's not sticking to the bottom. If the chicken is sticking, simply stir it to release it from the bottom. Next, add the peas to the pot and continue to cook for additional 5 minutes. Once the peas are heated through, turn off the heat.

Preheat your oven to 400°F (204°C). Spray four 4-inch (10-cm) wide cocottes with non-stick cooking spray. You could also use six ramekins or a 13 x 9-inch (33 x 23-cm) casserole dish. For the casserole, you won't cut the puff pastry. Simply place the entire sheet on top of the filled baking dish.

Ladle the chicken mixture into the cocottes, filling each about three-quarters of the way. Lay the puff pastry sheet on your countertop. Cut the puff pastry into four 4 x 4-inch (10 x 10-cm) squares. Place one of the puff pastry squares on top of the cocotte. In a small bowl, whisk the egg. Using a pastry brush, brush the top of the puff pastry with the egg wash. Using a paring knife, make a small 'x' in the middle of the puff pastry to help some of the steam escape. Repeat this process with the other cocottes.

Place the cocottes on a baking sheet. Bake the pot pies for about 15 minutes or until the tops are golden brown. Remove the baking sheet from the oven and let the pot pies cool for a couple of minutes before serving!

TWICE-BAKED CHICKEN SHAWARMA STUFFED POTATOES

Baked potatoes have been getting the shaft lately. The sexier, better-for-you sweet potato has been the center of attention. I get it. But Sir Russet's got some good things goin' on too, ya' know? He's got plenty of nutrients, and he's the perfect candidate for being stuffed or topped with extras. Speaking of extras, here's an unexpected one: chicken shawarma. Seriously. I've been eating and loving varieties of this Middle Eastern dish since I was a little girl, and yep—you can put it in a potato. A mixture of spices like cardamom, cumin, coriander and paprika give the chicken a little extra kick. Stuff it inside a baked potato and top it with fresh tomatoes, cucumbers and Greek yogurt, and you'll remember what made the standard issue potato so popular in the first place.

YIELDS 8 POTATOES

1 lb (450 g) thinly sliced boneless, skinless chicken thighs

1 tbsp (9 g) garlic powder

1 tbsp (9 g) ground cardamom

1 tbsp (9 g) ground cumin

1 tbsp (9 g) ground coriander

1 tbsp (9 g) ground paprika

1¼ tsp (9 g) kosher salt, divided

1¼ tsp (4 g) ground pepper, divided

¼ cup (60 ml) olive oil

2 tbsp (30 ml) lemon juice

4 russet potatoes

1 tbsp (14 g) clarified butter (page 183)

1 cup (285 g) plain Greek yogurt

1 cup (113 g) shredded mild cheddar cheese, divided

¼ cup (38 g) crumbled feta cheese

3 tbsp (42 g) unsalted butter

⅓ cup (80 ml) whole milk

Halved grape tomatoes, for garnish

Fresh mint, for garnish

Kitchen Tip: If you have any remaining potato mixture, just reheat and add as a side to any dinner meal!

In a large resealable plastic bag, add the chicken thighs, garlic powder, cardamom, cumin, coriander, paprika, 1 teaspoon of kosher salt, 1 teaspoon of ground pepper, olive oil and lemon juice. Close the bag and massage the chicken, making sure it's well coated with all the ingredients. Place the bag in the fridge to marinate for at least 4 hours or overnight.

Preheat the oven to 450°F (232°C). Take a potato and lightly prick holes into the skin using a fork. Place the potatoes on a small baking sheet that has been sprayed with non-stick cooking spray. Place the sheet into the oven and bake for 25 minutes. Remove the potatoes from the oven, flip them and continue to cook for an additional 20 to 25 minutes. Remove the baking sheet from the oven and set the potatoes aside to cool completely. Turn the oven down to 350°F (177°C).

Meanwhile, as the potatoes cool, preheat a large skillet to medium-high heat. Add the clarified butter and the chicken shawarma. Sauté the chicken until it is golden brown, or for about 6 minutes. Remove the chicken from the skillet using a pair of tongs and place it on a plate, then roughly chop into bite-sized pieces.

Now that the potatoes have cooled, take a potato and, with a sharp knife, slice the potato in half. Using a spoon, carefully scoop out the middle of the potato and place it into a mixing bowl, while leaving about a ¼-inch (0.6-cm) border along the sides. Place the potato halves cut-side-up on a new baking sheet. Add the Greek yogurt, ½ cup (57 g) of cheddar cheese and the feta to the bowl with the potato innards.

In small saucepan, preheated to medium heat, melt the butter and then gently add the milk. Stir to combine and heat through. Add the butter and milk mixture to the mixing bowl with the potatoes and, using a potato masher, mash until the mixture is smooth. Next, stir in ¼ teaspoon of salt, ¼ teaspoon of pepper and half of the chicken shawarma. Take the potato mixture and spoon it into each potato half. Top each half with the remaining chicken shawarma and ½ cup (57 g) of cheddar cheese. Place the potatoes into the oven and bake them for about 20 minutes or until the filling has heated through and the cheese is golden brown.

Garnish the potatoes with tomatoes, cucumbers, fresh mint and feta!

MUMBAI SHRIMP TACOS *with* AVOCADO SALSA

Mr. B and I are #tacotuesday enthusiasts. From a meal-planning perspective, taco Tuesday is brilliant because it's one less weekday evening meal to plan for. It also gives me a chance to mix things up from our standard pork or turkey tacos, and incorporate fish. Living in a land-locked state, sourcing great-tasting fish that won't break the Monopoly bank can be rather difficult. If I'm going to purchase fish on Park Avenue, you can bet your sweet tookus I'm going to make something sassy like these Mumbai Shrimp Tacos with Avocado Salsa. I love the simplicity of this dish because it incorporates few ingredients, but provides big flavor. Turmeric, paprika, coriander, cumin and garlic powder give these tacos just the right amount of spice. Topped with a simple avocado salsa, these will be right at home in your #tacotuesday rotation!

YIELDS 8 TACOS

1 tsp turmeric

1 tsp ground paprika

1 tsp ground coriander

1 tsp ground cumin

1 tsp garlic powder

2 tsp (12 g) kosher salt, divided

1 tsp ground pepper

1lb (454 g) shrimp, peeled and deveined

1 tbsp (14 g) clarified butter (page 183)

2 avocados, chopped

1½ cups (224 g) halved grape tomatoes

3 tbsp (45 ml) lime juice

2 cloves garlic, minced

1 jalapeño, seeded, minced

¼ cup (4 g) chopped cilantro

3 tbsp (45 ml) olive oil

8 (6-inch [15-cm]) taco-size soft tortillas, toasted

Lime wedges, for garnish

In a large mixing bowl, combine the turmeric, paprika, coriander, garlic powder, 1 teaspoon of kosher salt and 1 teaspoon of ground pepper. Add the shrimp to the bowl with the spices and toss to combine.

Preheat a large skillet to medium-high heat. Add the clarified butter and shrimp. Cook the shrimp for about a minute, flip and cook for an additional minute or until the shrimp start to curl and become golden brown. Remove the shrimp from the skillet and set it aside on a plate.

Mix together the avocado, grape tomatoes, lime juice, garlic, jalapeño, cilantro, olive oil and 1 teaspoon of the kosher salt.

To assemble the tacos, take a few pieces of shrimp and place them into the tortilla. Top with some avocado salsa and more lime juice!

Kitchen Tip: The shrimp and avocado salsa make for great toppings to any plate of nachos!

BACON & KIMCHI MAC & CHEESE

Mac and cheese should be used as a peace offering in international affairs. Am I right? I can't think of a skirmish that couldn't be settled over a giant bowl of noodles and perfectly gooey cheese. It's a hall-of-fame comfort food that brings a smile to even the grumpiest of personalities. I use this Bacon and Kimchi Mac and Cheese as my own personal olive branch when the going gets rough. Kimchi adds a crunch and warmth to this classic comfort dish. Make it once and they'll call you the peacemaker.

SERVES 6

5 slices bacon

½ lb (227 g) elbow macaroni

5 tbsp (70 g) unsalted butter, divided

4 tbsp (31 g) all-purpose flour

2¼ cups (540 ml) whole milk

1¾ cups (211 g) shredded medium cheddar cheese

¼ tsp kosher salt

¼ tsp ground pepper

⅔ cup (100 g) chopped kimchi

¾ cup (70 g) panko

1 tsp cayenne pepper

Preheat the oven to 400°F (204°C). Coat a baking sheet with non-stick cooking spray. Place the bacon on the baking sheet and bake it for about 12 to 15 minutes, or until crispy. Remove the bacon from the baking sheet and set it on a plate lined with a paper towel. Once it has cooled, roughly chop the bacon.

Bring a large pot of water to a boil. Cook the pasta according to package directions. Drain it and set it aside.

In another large pot, melt 4 tablespoons (56 g) of butter over medium-high heat. Add the flour and continue to whisk, creating a roux. Gradually add the milk and whisk until the sauce thickens, or about 5 minutes. Next, add the cheddar cheese and whisk until everything is completely smooth. Add the kosher salt, ground pepper, chopped bacon, kimchi and cooked pasta. Stir until everything is well combined. Pour the mixture into a 13 x 9-inch (33 x 23-cm) baking dish. Add the remaining 1 tablespoon (14 g) of butter to a microwave safe bowl and melt the butter. In the bowl with the melted butter, stir in the panko and cayenne. Sprinkle the panko mixture in an even layer over the mac and cheese. Bake the mac and cheese for about 10 to 15 minutes or until it is golden brown.

Kitchen Tip: If you're purchasing store-bought kimchi make sure to open the jar over the sink. Kimchi naturally builds pressure, kind of like champagne. Using a paper towel, slowly twist open the lid, releasing the pressure.

ASIAN-STYLE SLOPPY JOES

The lunch lady is one gal kids never want to cross. Play nice and you might get seconds. Get sassy and your plate might look like an army ration. A close relationship with the cafeteria queen can pay off big-time, especially on sloppy joes day, when a second scoop of messy ground round is a ticket to little-kid lunch heaven. Asian-Style Sloppy Joes are old-school meets new-school. The sloppy joe vehicle stays the same, but it's paired with a spicy kick from the chili garlic sauce, ginger and hoisin. You'll want to make a double batch because everybody will jump in line for seconds!

SERVES 4

2 tbsp (28 g) clarified butter (page 183)

1 cup (150 g) chopped yellow onion

2 tbsp (29 ml) chili garlic sauce

1 tbsp (6 g) freshly grated ginger

1 clove garlic, minced

1 tsp kosher salt

1 tsp ground pepper

1 lb (450 g) ground chicken thighs, or ground pork

½ cup (118 ml) hoisin sauce

1 tbsp (15 ml) soy sauce

½ cup (100 g) drained, canned, fire-roasted tomatoes

1 tbsp (15 ml) lime juice

4 brioche buns, toasted

Raw broccoli slaw, for garnish

Shredded Napa cabbage, for garnish

In a large skillet preheated to medium-high heat, add the clarified butter, followed by the onion, garlic sauce, ginger, garlic clove, kosher salt and ground pepper. Sauté the veggies, stirring often until they are softened, or about 5 minutes.

Next, add the ground chicken to the skillet, breaking up the chicken with a wooden spoon. Cook the chicken until it is no longer pink, or for about 6 minutes. Then stir in the hoisin, soy sauce, tomatoes and lime juice. Bring the mixture to a boil and then a simmer over low heat for about 20 minutes, or until the sauce has thickened.

Once the sauce is at your desired consistency, ladle some of the sloppy joe mixture on top of a brioche bun bottom. To give the sloppy joe some crunch, top it with raw broccoli slaw and/or Napa cabbage and top it with the remaining bun. Repeat the process until all the sloppy joes have been assembled!

Kitchen Tip: These sloppy joes will stay fresh in the fridge for up to three days. Simply make ahead and reheat when you have a craving or need to feed an army.

TURKISH BURGER *with* FATTOUSH LIME SLAW

I grew up in middle America—you would think I'd have a hard time finding access to ethnic food, right? Actually, I was eating Vietnamese, Mexican and Lebanese food all before hitting my teens. I will never forget the first time I took a bite of a fattoush salad. Crisp romaine, pita croutons, tomatoes and cucumbers dressed in a lime vinaigrette—it was strange and wonderful and zesty like no salad I'd ever tasted. This Turkish Burger with Fattoush Lime Slaw is a nod to that past education. Juicy, spiced lamb is topped with a fattoush slaw as zesty as that early memory. Hopefully, this burger becomes something you remember and return to, too.

SERVES 4

FATTOUSH LIME SLAW

½ cup (120 ml) olive oil

1 tsp ground sumac

½ tsp ground cinnamon

¼ tsp allspice

1 clove garlic, minced

3 tbsp (45 ml) fresh lime juice

½ tsp kosher salt

¼ tsp ground pepper

2½ cups (250 g) thinly sliced Napa cabbage

TURKISH BURGER

1½ lb (680 g) ground lamb

1 tsp ground oregano

1 tbsp (4 g) chopped fresh mint

½ tsp ground cinnamon

½ tsp ground cardamom

½ tsp ground paprika

½ tsp ground cumin

½ tsp kosher salt

¼ tsp ground pepper

1 clove garlic, minced

3 tbsp (45 ml) olive oil, divided

4 hamburger buns

Crumbled feta, for garnish

Tomato slices, for garnish

Cucumber slices, for garnish

FOR THE FATTOUSH LIME SLAW

In a large bowl, whisk together the olive oil, sumac, cinnamon, allspice, garlic, lime juice, kosher salt and ground pepper. Add the Napa cabbage and gently toss it with the spices. Place the bowl in the fridge for at least 30 minutes to let the flavors combine.

FOR THE TURKISH BURGER

In a large bowl, add the ground lamb, oregano, mint, cinnamon, cardamom, paprika, cumin, kosher salt, ground pepper, garlic and 1 tablespoon (15 ml) of olive oil. Mix all the ingredients together and divide the lamb into 4 fist-sized hamburger patties.

In a cast-iron skillet preheated to medium-high heat, add 2 tablespoons (30 ml) of olive oil. Add the lamb patties to the skillet and cook them for about 4 to 6 minutes on the first side, flip, and continue to cook for another 4 to 6 minutes, or until slightly pink inside. Remove the lamb patties from the skillet and place them on a cutting board to rest for a few minutes before serving. To assemble the burger, place a lamb patty on the bottom of a bun. Top it with feta, tomato, cucumber and fattoush lime slaw. Add the top of the bun and repeat the process until the other burgers have been assembled.

Variation: Have fun mixing up the slaw by trying radicchio, red cabbage or even shredded Brussels sprouts!

SLOW COOKER CHINESE BOLOGNESE

For the longest time I was scared of my slow cooker. Why? I haven't a darn clue. I've got an older model, and it has an old-school, creepy kind of vibe. Come closer, Lauren . . . let your dear old slow cooker get a good look at you. Yikes! Turns out I was wasting time, though, because my slow cooker has become one of the most useful gadgets I own. I probably use the old gal about three times a week, I'd bet. The latest addition to my slow-cooking routine is this Slow Cooker Chinese Bolognese. It's similar to Italian bolognese, but with a peppy Asian kick. Chili garlic sauce, soy sauce, balsamic vinegar, coriander, garlic and beef short ribs are slowly cooked to make a luxurious sauce. Top it with noodles for an easy-to-repeat addition to your dinner repertoire.

SERVES 4

2 cups (475 ml) low sodium beef stock

4 tsp (28 g) white miso

4 tsp (28 g) Sriracha, plus more for garnish

2 tbsp (30 ml) hoisin

2 tbsp (30 ml) low sodium soy sauce

4 tsp (20 ml) balsamic vinegar

2 tsp (8 g) brown sugar

1 tsp toasted sesame oil

1 tbsp (14 g) clarified butter (page 183)

8 beef short ribs

1½ tsp (9 g) kosher salt, divided

1½ tsp (4 g) ground pepper, divided

1 cup (152 g) chopped carrots

1 cup (101 g) chopped celery

1 cup (150 g) chopped yellow onion

1 clove garlic, minced

1 tbsp (6 g) chopped fresh ginger

14 oz (400 g) soba or udon noodles

Scallions, sliced, for garnish

In a medium bowl, combine the beef stock, miso, Sriracha, hoisin, soy sauce, balsamic vinegar, brown sugar and toasted sesame oil.

In a large skillet preheated to medium-high heat, add the clarified butter, short ribs, ½ teaspoon of kosher salt and ½ teaspoon of the ground pepper. Sear the short ribs for about 3 minutes, flip and season the other side with another ½ teaspoon of kosher salt and ½ teaspoon of ground pepper. Sear the short ribs for another 2 minutes and then remove the ribs from the skillet and set them into the bottom of the slow cooker.

Remove all but 1 tablespoon (15 ml) of excess fat. Next, add the carrots, celery, onion, garlic, ginger, ½ teaspoon of kosher salt and ½ teaspoon of ground pepper. Sauté the veggies until they have slightly softened, or for about 4 minutes. Add the veggies to the slow cooker, followed by the sauce. Set the slow cooker to high for 4 hours or on low for 8 hours, checking halfway through the cooking process that there is enough liquid. If not, simply add more beef stock, as needed.

Prepare your noodles according to the package instructions. Once the noodles have cooked, divide them among four bowls. Remove the short ribs from the slow cooker and place on a cutting board. Discard the bone and roughly chop the beef. Ladle some of the bolognese over the top of the noodles followed by the chopped beef. Garnish with scallions and more Sriracha.

THAI CHICKEN & RICE CASSEROLE

Chicken and rice casserole is a classic. The loaded, condensed soup–based casserole is straight out of the pages of a 1950s Junior League cookbook. It was easy to assemble, could feed an army and was somewhat healthy because of the lean chicken breasts. Well, my thirty-four-year-old-self took one look at those cringe-worthy, old and yellowed food photos and decided it was time to upgrade. Meet the modern version: Thai Chicken & Rice Casserole. A blend of Thai flavors takes the place of the condensed soup base. Add in brown rice and chicken thighs or breasts, and you and your seven-year-old self will be high-fiving!

SERVES 4 TO 6

2 tbsp (30 ml) red curry paste

2 tbsp (30 ml) chili garlic sauce

2 tbsp (11 g) freshly grated ginger

2 cloves garlic, grated

6 tbsp (84 g) unsalted butter

6 tbsp (54 g) all-purpose flour

1 cup (245 ml) whole milk

2 cups (480 ml) chicken stock

1 tbsp (15 ml) olive oil

½ cup (75 g) chopped orange bell pepper

½ cup (149 g) chopped yellow onion

½ tsp kosher salt

½ tsp ground pepper

1 cup (158 g) uncooked long grain rice

1 lb (450 g) boneless, skinless chicken thighs, cut into 1-inch (2.5-cm) cubes

Fresh cilantro, for garnish

Sriracha, for garnish

Preheat the oven to 375°F (191°C). Spray a 13 x 9-inch (33 x 23-cm) baking dish with non-stick cooking spray and set aside.

In a small bowl, combine the curry paste, chili garlic sauce, ginger and garlic. In a medium saucepan preheated to medium-heat, melt the butter. Add 1 tablespoon (37 g) of the Thai mixture and stir to combine it with the butter. Next, add the flour and continue to whisk until a roux forms. The roux will be slightly brown and thickened. Pour in the milk and begin to whisk. Continue whisking as you pour in the chicken stock. Bring the sauce to a slight simmer and stir the sauce continuously until it has thickened, or for about 5 minutes.

As the sauce mixture thickens, preheat a small skillet to medium-high heat. Add the olive oil, orange pepper, yellow onion, kosher salt and ground pepper. Sauté the veggies until they are softened, or for about 4 to 5 minutes. Once the veggies are cooked, add them to a large mixing bowl.

Once the sauce has thickened, pour the sauce mixture into the large mixing bowl with the veggies and add the uncooked rice. Stir until everything is well combined.

Pour the mixture into the prepared baking dish. Add the chicken to a small mixing bowl and toss with the remaining Thai mixture. Place the chicken on top of the rice mixture and cover the baking dish with foil. Bake for about 30 to 40 minutes. Remove the dish from the oven and allow it cool slightly before serving. Garnish with cilantro and Sriracha!

Kitchen Tip: If you prefer to use boneless chicken breasts instead of thighs, add the chicken breasts during the last 20 minutes of cooking!

ASIAN DEVILED EGGS

We all have a weakness for deviled eggs, right? At my house they were an Easter Sunday tradition, and as a little girl I'd wait patiently for my mother to put out that tray of slightly over-boiled egg whites stuffed with yolk, mayo, mustard, vinegar and the traditional dusting of paprika. If they're so scrumptious, why eat them but once a year? This recipe gives the standard-issue deviled egg an eastern twist: mayonnaise, chili garlic sauce, soy sauce and honey make for a killer appetizer all year round.

YIELDS 12 EGGS

6 large eggs

½ tsp white wine vinegar

⅓ cup (77 g) mayonnaise

1 tbsp (15 ml) chili garlic sauce

1 tsp hoisin sauce

1 tsp soy sauce

1 tsp honey

⅛ tsp salt

⅛ tsp pepper

Scallions, sliced, for garnish

Place the eggs in the bottom of a large pot. Fill the pot with cold water, covering the eggs. Bring the water to a full boil and add the white wine vinegar. Turn off the heat and cover the pot and let the eggs sit for about 10 to 12 minutes. Strain the water from the pot and run cold water over the eggs to stop the cooking. Place the eggs in a bowl and begin to peel away the shell. If the eggshell is being stubborn, hold the egg under the faucet and, while the cold water is running, gently use your fingers to remove the shell.

Once all the eggshells have been removed, slice the eggs in half and scoop the cooked yolk into a large bowl. Mash the egg yolks and add the mayonnaise, chili garlic sauce, hoisin sauce, soy sauce, honey, salt and pepper. Stir to completely combine. Spoon a heaping teaspoon of the mixture into each halved egg. Garnish the eggs with sliced scallions.

Kitchen Tip: Let the filling sit in an airtight container for at least 4 hours or overnight to maximize the flavor!

LEBANESE MARGHERITA LAMB PIZZA

I make a lot of Middle Eastern dishes during the work week. Spices like cumin, coriander, sumac, cardamom, cinnamon, paprika and cloves turn any chicken and rice dish into an $^{11}/_{10}$ situation. Can you say "winning"? The spices do all the work, and that's the case with this Margherita Lamb Pizza, too. It's a red-sauced pizza topped with lamb, and mixed with the traditional Lebanese seven spices. Cover this bad boy in cheese, bake and you'll get over that mid-week hump with ease.

SERVES 4

2 tbsp (30 ml) olive oil, divided

2 cloves garlic, grated

1 lb (450 g) ground lamb

2 tsp (6 g) ground cumin

2 tsp (6 g) ground coriander

½ tsp ground cloves

½ tsp ground nutmeg

¼ tsp ground cinnamon

¼ tsp ground cardamon

1 tsp kosher salt

1 tsp ground pepper

4 pieces whole wheat naan

1⅓ cups (317 ml) marinara sauce

8 tomato slices

⅓ cups (148 g) shredded mozzarella cheese

Fresh basil, for garnish

Red pepper flakes, garnish

Preheat the oven to 425°F (218°C).

In a small bowl, combine 1 tablespoon (15 ml) of the olive oil and the garlic and set it aside. Meanwhile, preheat a skillet to medium-high heat and add the remaining 1 tablespoon (15 ml) of olive oil. Next, add the lamb, cumin, coriander, cloves, nutmeg, cinnamon, cardamom, kosher salt and ground pepper. Using a wooden spoon, break up the ground lamb and incorporate all the spices. Continue to cook the lamb until it is no longer pink, or for about 5 minutes.

Spray two baking sheets with non-stick cooking spray. Place 2 pieces of the naan on each baking sheet. Using a pastry brush, brush the garlic olive oil over the top of each naan. Next, spread ⅓ cup (80 ml) of marinara sauce on top of the garlic olive oil, leaving a thin border. Top the marinara with ground lamb followed by two tomato slices and ⅓ cup (35 g) of mozzarella. Repeat this process until all of the naan have been covered. Place the baking sheets into the oven to bake for about 12 to 15 minutes, or until the cheese is golden brown. Remove the baking sheets from the oven and let the naan cool slightly before slicing. Garnish with fresh basil and red pepper flakes.

Variation: Is your grocery store out of lamb? Ground beef, ground chicken thighs or ground pork makes a great substitute. Or to make this dish vegetarian, try using chickpeas!

FRENCH ONION UDON NOODLE SOUP

French onion soup is making a hearty, cheesy comeback. This meat-flavored soup stock is traditionally mixed with sultry caramelized onions, buttered croutons and copious amounts of cheese—no wonder we're welcoming it back to the comfort food circle of love! And now that this classy French lady is back in action, why not give her a little makeover? Instead of a heavy roux base, I'm giving Mademoiselle a sexy new noodle to try on: the udon. A thick, wheat-flour noodle used in Japanese cuisine, this noodle gives French Onion Soup the modern touch. This recipe is easy to assemble, and worth every slurp. Bon appetite!

SERVES 4

4 tbsp (56 g) unsalted butter

3 cups (450 g) thinly sliced yellow onions

1 tsp kosher salt

1 tsp ground pepper

3 tsp (15 g) granulated sugar

1½ tbsp (20 ml) Worcestershire sauce

3 tsp (1 g) chopped fresh thyme

6 cups (1.4 L) beef broth, divided

½ lb (227 g) fresh udon noodles, roughly chopped

1 cup (100 g) grated fontina cheese

In a large Dutch oven preheated to medium heat, melt the butter. Place the onions into the Dutch oven and let them sweat for about 3 to 4 minutes. Add the kosher salt, ground pepper, sugar, Worcestershire sauce and fresh thyme. Stir and cook for another couple of minutes then add 1 cup (240 ml) of the beef broth and cook until the onions are golden brown, or for about 20 minutes. Remove the skillet from the heat and set it aside.

Meanwhile, in a large pot, bring the remaining 5 cups (1.2 L) of the beef broth to a boil. Add the udon noodles and cook them according to the package instructions. Once the udon noodles are cooked, add them along with the beef broth to the Dutch oven with the onions. Stir to combine, adding more thyme if needed. Divide the noodle soup among four bowls and top the soup with fontina cheese.

Variation: If you can't find udon noodles at your grocery store, try using ramen noodles. Simply omit the seasoning packet and add the ramen noodles where the udon noodles are specified!

Ultimate Mash-Ups

I was the kid in school who stirred everything together.

When the lunch bell rang, I would bolt down the long brick hallway to the cafeteria in hopes of being the first in line. Fried chicken, mashed potatoes and gravy and buttered corn day came but once a month. I'd grab my khaki-colored lunch tray with a one-handed swoop and make it just in time to be—shucks—third, in line.

As I would anxiously wait for my tray to be filled by the lovely lunch ladies in their blue polyester uniforms, I could hear my stomach grumble. "Do you want corn, peas or carrots, my dear?" the lunch lady would ask, in her scratchy voice. I was so hungry, I wanted them all! But I'd snap out my hunger fog and give her an answer: "I'll have corn, please."

With a quick plop and slap my glorious lunch plate would be formed. I carefully strolled to the lunch tables, careful not to spill anything, then gently set the tray on the laminate table and smiled. What happens next is a "sectional eater's" worst nightmare. I'd take a fork and begin to mix the chicken, mashed potatoes and gravy and corn. I stirred and stirred, until the mound of mixture was distributed evenly. Then I stuck in my fork and took a giant bite. My seven-year-old foodie dreams had come true!

I believe my love for food mash-ups started back in the stirring-frenzy of my cafeteria days. Today, I still love to combine food—as if I were a scientist forming an experiment in my kitchen. These mash-ups are made to be fun and shared with others, and to get you thinking differently about the way food is supposed to be eaten. Plus, each recipe is super delicious! Make sure to try the Easy Cuban Caesar Salad (page 88), Shepherd's Pie Poutine (page 83) and Lamb Curry Gnocchi (page 76). These dishes are *made* to be stirred up!

STEAK & EGG BREAKFAST PIZZA

Brunch is more than just a meal in our household—it's a ceremony. Every Saturday or Sunday morning we venture out to a local restaurant where we sit down to a scrumptious meal, catch up on the latest news and sip coffee, all before thinking about the weekend chore list. When it comes to brunch, we're on "team savory," and nothing is off-limits. This twist on classic steak and eggs features perfectly seared steak, thinly sliced and placed atop fresh, homemade pizza that's covered in a white sauce and topped with eggs. This pizza is perfect for lunch and dinner, too.

SERVES 4

PIZZA DOUGH

1½ cups (360 ml) flat beer

3¾ cups (450 g) all-purpose flour

3 tbsp (38 g) granulated sugar

1½ tsp (17 g) kosher salt

1½ tsp (5 ml) olive oil

1½ tsp (17 g) quick-rise, active yeast

WHITE SAUCE

2 tbsp (28 g) unsalted butter

2 cloves garlic, minced

1 shallot, diced

2 tbsp (30 ml) white wine

½ cup (119 ml) heavy cream

⅓ cup (27 g) shredded Parmesan cheese

Salt and pepper, to taste

STEAK

1 tbsp (14 g) unsalted butter

1 (6-oz [170-g]) boneless ribeye steak

1 tbsp (15 ml) olive oil

Salt and pepper, to taste

ASSEMBLY

3 to 4 large eggs

1¼ cups (141 g) shredded mozzarella cheese

Chopped chives, for garnish

Preheat the oven to 400°F (204°C).

FOR THE PIZZA DOUGH

In a large bowl, combine the beer, flour, sugar, kosher salt, olive oil and yeast. Stir this mixture until it begins to hold together. The dough will be sticky. Turn the dough out onto a floured surface and knead it for about 10 minutes. Add additional flour as needed to prevent the dough from sticking. Once the dough is soft and pliable, form the dough into a ball and place the dough in a lightly-oiled bowl. Cover the bowl with plastic wrap or a towel and set it aside in a warm area to rise until it doubles in size, about 45 to 55 minutes. After the dough has risen, remove it from the bowl and place it on the floured surface. Divide the dough into two pieces and save one piece for another use. Roll out the dough into a 12-inch (30-cm) round to fit a sheet pan. Spread a thin layer of olive oil over the surface of the sheet pan and place the dough onto the pan.

FOR THE WHITE SAUCE

Preheat a medium saucepan to medium-high heat. Melt the unsalted butter and add the garlic, shallot, salt and pepper. Sauté until the shallot has softened, or about 2 to 3 minutes. Next, add the white wine and let the shallot simmer for a few minutes until the alcohol cooks out. Add the cream and the Parmesan. Stir to combine, and reduce the heat slightly until the sauce is slightly thickened, about 2 minutes.

FOR THE STEAK

Preheat a cast-iron skillet to medium-high heat and melt the unsalted butter. Drizzle both sides of the steak with the olive oil, salt and pepper. Pan-grill the steak for about 3 minutes on each side for medium-rare. Once grilled, remove the steak and let it rest on a plate before slicing it thinly.

TO ASSEMBLE THE PIZZA

Once you've rolled out your dough onto a baking sheet, spread the white sauce evenly across the top of the dough, leaving a 1-inch (3-cm) border. Next, sprinkle the pizza with ½ cup (56 g) of the mozzarella, followed by the steak slices. Place the pizza in the oven and bake it for 15 minutes. Remove the pizza from the oven and carefully crack the eggs over the pizza. Sprinkle the top of the pizza with the remaining mozzarella. Bake the pizza until it is golden brown and the eggs are cooked to your liking, or about 5 to 10 additional minutes. Remove the pizza from the oven and let it rest for about 5 to 7 minutes before serving. Sprinkle the top of the pizza with chives, slice and serve.

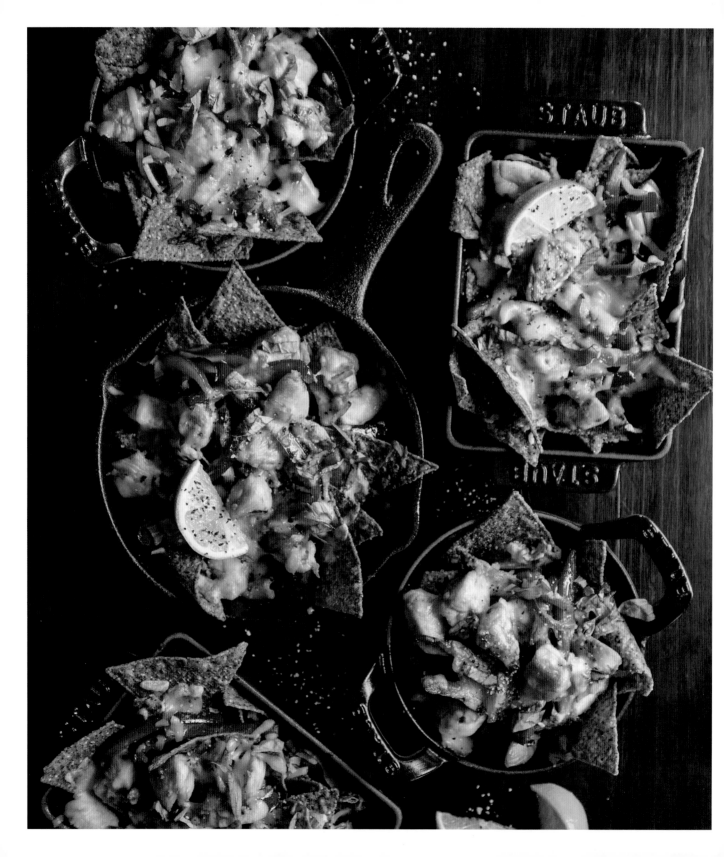

THAI CHICKEN STIR-FRY SKILLET NACHOS

Mr. B and I like to play a little game on weeknights when we don't want to cook. The game is called, simply, "What you got?" We literally open the fridge and pull out leftover ingredients to create our dinner. True, some of these impromptu dinners have left us scratching our heads, or plugging our noses just to get it all down. But others, like the Thai Chicken Stir-Fry Skillet Nachos here, kept our faith and trust alive in "What you got?" These nachos are a brilliant smash-up of Thai chicken stir-fry and cheesy nachos. Spiced coconut sauce and sautéed chicken are poured over crisp tortilla chips, making for a killer weeknight dinner or a perfect excuse for an impromptu party!

SERVES 4

⅓ cup (80 ml) unsweetened coconut milk

1 tbsp (15 ml) fish sauce

1 tbsp (15 ml) soy sauce

1 tbsp (15 ml) fresh lime juice

¼ tsp red pepper flakes

1 tsp (7 g) brown sugar

1 lb (450 g) chicken breast, cut into bite-size pieces about ¼-inch (6-mm) thick

1 tbsp (15 ml) olive oil

2 cloves garlic, minced

1 cup (100 g) thinly sliced red bell pepper

½ cup (65 g) thinly sliced red onion

1 tbsp (6 g) freshly minced ginger

¼ cup (16 g) chopped fresh basil

4 cups (136 g) blue corn tortilla chips

1 cup (125 g) shredded mozzarella cheese

1 cup (125 g) shredded mild cheddar cheese

In a medium bowl, combine the coconut milk, fish sauce, soy sauce, lime juice, red pepper flakes and brown sugar. Add the chicken to the mixture and stir to combine. Let this mixture stand at room temperature for 30 minutes.

Preheat a large skillet to medium-high heat and add the olive oil. Remove the chicken from the coconut milk mixture and place it in the skillet. Sauté the chicken for about 2 to 3 minutes. Add the coconut liquid to the skillet and reduce it for a few minutes. Next, add the garlic and cook it for another minute. Finally, add the red pepper, red onion and ginger. Sauté the chicken and vegetables for 5 minutes or until the veggies are crisp and the chicken is no longer pink inside. Toss in the basil and stir.

Next, preheat the broiler. Add the blue corn chips to a 10-inch (25-cm) cast-iron skillet. Or if you want to serve it for a party, divide the mixture between a few 6-inch (15-cm) mini cast-iron skillets. Using a slotted spoon, add the Thai chicken stir-fry on top of the tortilla chips making sure the chicken is evenly distributed. Top the Thai chicken with mozzarella and cheddar cheese. Place the skillet under the broiler for a few minutes or until the cheese is golden brown.

Kitchen Tip: When using coconut milk, pour the milk out of the can into a small bowl. Mix it well to ensure that the coconut solids and the liquid are completely combined. Once combined, measure the mixture as needed.

LAMB CURRY GNOCCHI

I love a good mash-up! Having experimented a lot in this area, it wasn't until I combined my go-to pasta (gnocchi) and my favorite takeout dish (curried lamb) that I finally found "the one." Making the curry is a cinch. Combine spices, lamb, sweet potatoes and coconut milk in a large pot and let them simmer away. The aroma is amazing, so be prepared to feed the neighbors. This stuff is at its best when ladled over a hearty starch, like the fluffy potato gnocchi gems I use here. You won't find this homecooked winner on a takeout menu.

SERVES 4

2 tbsp (28 g) clarified butter (page 183)

1 cup (150 g) diced yellow onion

2 cloves garlic, minced

1 tbsp (6 g) minced fresh ginger

1 tsp kosher salt, divided

1 tsp ground pepper, divided

1 lb (450 g) ground lamb

2 cups (400 g) cubed sweet potato

1 (14-oz [397-g]) can unsweetened coconut milk

¾ cup (178 ml) chicken stock

2 tbsp (30 g) curry powder

1 cup (150 g) frozen peas

1 (12-oz [300-g]) package dried gnocchi

Fresh mint, for garnish

Fresh cilantro, for garnish

In a large skillet preheated to medium-high heat, add the clarified butter. Next, add the onion, garlic, ginger, ½ teaspoon of the kosher salt and ½ teaspoon of the ground pepper. Sauté until the onions have softened, or for about 4 minutes.

Add the ground lamb and break it up with a wooden spoon. Cook the lamb until it is no longer pink, or about 5 minutes. Next, add in the sweet potatoes, milk, chicken stock, curry powder, ½ teaspoon of kosher salt and ½ teaspoon of ground pepper. Bring the mixture to a boil and then simmer it, covered, for about 15 minutes. Add the peas and simmer for an additional 5 minutes.

While the curry cooks, bring a large pot of water to a boil. Cook the gnocchi according to the package directions. Drain the gnocchi and divide the gnocchi among four bowls. Once the curry has cooked, ladle the mixture over the gnocchi and serve it with the fresh mint and cilantro.

Kitchen Tip: Make this dish a day ahead. The longer the flavors sit, the better the curry will taste!

Variation: Ground chicken or beef can be substituted for the lamb. Also, chimichurri is a fabulous garnish to dollop on the top of this curry!

FALAFEL WAFFLE

Falafel Waffle. Is that not the most fun thing to say? And not only is it fun to say, it's also super fun to eat! Falafel Waffle is exactly what it sounds like. Form a falafel patty with the usual suspects—chickpeas, onion, garlic, cumin, cilantro and parsley. Take the falafel and pat it down inside a hot waffle-maker and poof! You have a perfectly golden Falafel Waffle in minutes. It's great for breakfast, lunch or dinner. And don't forget the cucumber tzatziki sauce, which I've touched-up with garlic—it's the pièce de résistance when it comes to making these waffles top-notch!

SERVES 2 TO 3

2 cups (470 g) plain Greek yogurt

1 cup (133 g) chopped cucumber

1 clove garlic, minced

1 tbsp (15 ml) lemon juice

1 tsp lemon zest

¼ cup (5 g) fresh dill

1½ tsp (8 g) kosher salt, divided

1½ tsp (3 g) ground pepper, divided

2 (15-oz [840-g]) cans of chickpeas, drained and rinsed

2 large eggs

2 tbsp (30 ml) olive oil

1 cup (150 g) roughly chopped yellow onion

3 cloves garlic, peeled

2 tsp (4 g) ground cumin

1 tsp coriander

¼ tsp cayenne

1 cup (16 g) packed parsley leaves

¼ cup (4 g) packed cilantro

2 tsp (4 g) baking powder

1½ cups (75 g) panko

Grape tomatoes, halved, for garnish

Crumbled feta, for garnish

To make the tzatziki sauce, in a medium mixing bowl, add the Greek yogurt, cucumber, minced garlic, lemon juice, lemon zest, dill, ½ teaspoon of kosher salt and ½ teaspoon of ground pepper. Stir to combine. Place the bowl in the fridge until it is ready to use.

To make the falafel, in a large food processor, add the chickpeas, eggs, olive oil, onion, garlic, cumin, coriander, cayenne, parsley, cilantro, baking powder, 1 teaspoon of kosher salt and 1 teaspoon of ground pepper. Pulse a few times until the ingredients are combined, scraping down the sides of the work bowl as needed. The mixture should be slightly chunky. Scrape the falafel mixture into a bowl and gently fold in the panko.

Heat your waffle iron and then spray it with non-stick cooking spray to keep the falafel from sticking. This recipe should make two waffles. Take the falafel mixture and scoop it onto the waffle iron. Spread the mixture into an even layer and then close the waffle iron lid. Cook the waffles until they are golden brown, or for about 3 to 5 minutes or longer, depending on your waffle iron. Remove the falafel waffle and set it on a plate. Repeat the process with the remaining falafel mixture. Garnish the waffles with the tzatziki sauce, grape tomatoes and feta.

Kitchen Tip: If you are using a Belgian waffle iron, about ⅓ cup (78 ml) of the falafel mixture will fit in each square.

CHICKEN CHEESESTEAK BAKED ZITI

Like most humans, I'm a fan of sandwiches smothered in cheese and peppers. The classic cheesesteak was a Philadelphia resident's stroke of genius: toasted sourdough bread stuffed with thinly-sliced chicken or beef, grilled peppers and onions, and layered with gooey provolone cheese—what more could one want? Well, have you ever tried a cheesesteak in a baked ziti kind of situation? This Chicken Cheesesteak Baked Ziti gives the classic sub a run for its money. Make the traditional chicken cheesesteak fixings, toss them with buttery ziti, top the pasta with an obscene amount of provolone cheese and bake! What you get is a comfort food mash-up that'll ring anybody's Liberty Bell.

SERVES 4 TO 6

PASTA
Pinch of salt

8 oz (227 g) dry ziti or rigatoni pasta

PEPPERS AND ONIONS
2 tbsp (28 g) clarified butter (page 183)

1 cup (130 g) thinly-sliced yellow onion

1 cup (110 g) thinly-sliced red pepper

1 cup (110 g) thinly-sliced green pepper

1 tsp kosher salt

1 tsp ground pepper

1 tbsp (53 ml) red wine vinegar

CHICKEN
2 tbsp (30 ml) olive oil

1 lb (450 g) boneless, skinless chicken breasts, thinly-sliced

1 tbsp (18 g) Italian seasoning

1 tsp kosher salt

1 tsp ground pepper

PROVOLONE SAUCE
4 tbsp (56 g) unsalted butter

4 tbsp (60 g) all-purpose flour

2 cups (480 ml) whole milk

1½ cups (150 g) shredded provolone cheese

1 tsp kosher salt

1 tsp ground pepper

6 slices provolone cheese

Fresh chopped parsley, for garnish

FOR THE PASTA
Fill a large pot with water and bring it to a boil. Add a pinch of kosher salt to the water, followed by the pasta. Cook the pasta according to package instructions or until al dente. Strain the pasta through a colander and pour it into a large mixing bowl.

FOR THE PEPPERS AND ONIONS
In a large skillet preheated to medium-high heat, add the clarified butter. Next, add the onion, red pepper, green pepper, kosher salt and ground pepper. Sauté the veggies until they are softened and golden brown, about 10 minutes. If you need to add water to the pan to prevent the veggies from sticking that's okay! Remove the skillet from the heat and stir in the red wine vinegar. Pour the peppers and onions into the bowl with the drained pasta.

FOR THE CHICKEN
In a large skillet preheated to medium-high heat, add the olive oil. Next, add the chicken breasts, along with the Italian seasoning, kosher salt and ground pepper. Toss everything together and sauté the chicken for about 8 minutes or until it is no longer pink inside. Remove the chicken from the skillet using a pair of tongs, and place it into the bowl with the pasta, peppers and onions.

FOR THE PROVOLONE SAUCE
In a medium saucepan preheated to medium heat, add the unsalted butter. Let it melt and then whisk in the flour. Keep whisking for a minute or until you cook out all of that raw flour taste. Gradually add the milk. Stir often so the mixture doesn't clump. After about 5 minutes the sauce should thicken, then add the provolone. Keep stirring, and season with salt and pepper. Turn off the heat and pour the sauce over the chicken, peppers, onions and pasta. Toss to make sure everything is well combined.

To assemble the dish, preheat the oven to 400°F (204°C). Spray a 13 x 9-inch (33 x 23-cm) baking dish with non-stick cooking spray. Pour the chicken cheesesteak mixture into the prepared baking dish. Top the chicken mixture with provolone slices and place the dish into the oven. Bake it for about 15 minutes or until the cheese is golden brown. Remove the chicken cheesesteak from the oven and garnish it with fresh chopped parsley.

SHEPHERD'S PIE POUTINE

Let's call this what it is: a match made in heaven! If you don't know what poutine is, I'll let you in on the details. Poutine is a Canadian comfort food comprised of French fries, cheese curds and a covering of brown gravy. Freakin' genius, right? If anyone knows how to cook soul-warming food to cure cold-weather blues, it's the Canadians. So here I've added a subtle touch by layering in a hearty shepherd's pie mix of ground beef, peas, carrots and Worcestershire sauce. Okay, so maybe it's not so subtle. French fries, cheese curds, shepherd's pie and poutine gravy—this is the ultimate comfort dish.

SERVES 4

FRIES
3 russet potatoes
Vegetable oil, for frying

POUTINE GRAVY
1 tbsp (15 ml) olive oil
¼ cup (25 g) minced shallot
1 clove garlic, minced
2 tbsp (28 g) unsalted butter
2 tbsp (18 g) all-purpose flour
3 cups (600 ml) beef stock
1 cup (240 ml) dark beer
2 tbsp (36 g) ketchup
1 tbsp (15 ml) apple cider vinegar
1½ tsp (8 ml) Worcestershire sauce
¼ tsp kosher salt
¼ tsp ground pepper

SHEPHERD'S PIE
1 tbsp (15 ml) olive oil
1 lb (450 g) lean ground beef
1 cup (182 g) vegetable mixture (peas, corn, carrots), either frozen or canned
¼ tsp kosher salt
¼ tsp ground pepper
1½ tsp (8 ml) Worcestershire sauce
½ cup (125 ml) beef broth
1 cup (113 g) white cheddar cheese curds

FOR THE FRIES

Peel the russet potatoes and cut them into a ¼-inch (6-mm) slices. Place the potato slices into a bowl filled with cold water. Cover the bowl with foil and let the potatoes soak for at least 2 hours or up to 24 hours at room temperature. Once the potatoes have fully soaked, remove the them from the water and place them on a baking sheet lined with a dish towel. Blot them dry to remove any excess water. Meanwhile, add oil to a Dutch oven, filling it about 2 inches (5 cm) high. Heat the oil using a frying thermometer to 350°F (177°C). Working in batches, fry the French fries until they are golden brown, or for about 3 to 4 minutes. Remove the fries from the Dutch oven and place them on a baking sheet lined with a paper towel. Repeat the process until all the potatoes have been fried.

FOR THE POUTINE GRAVY

In a medium saucepan preheated to medium heat, add the olive oil, shallot and garlic clove. Sauté the shallot and garlic for about 2 to 3 minutes or until they are softened. Next, add the butter and stir until it is melted. Add the flour and stir constantly with a wooden spoon for 1 to 2 minutes. This will cook out any raw flour taste and allow the sauce to become thick. You have now created a roux! Once the roux has thickened, very slowly whisk in the beef stock, beer, ketchup, apple cider vinegar and Worcestershire sauce. Whisk to combine. Simmer the gravy for about 10 to 12 minutes, or until it is reduced by half and is slightly thickened. Add ¼ teaspoon of kosher salt and ¼ teaspoon of ground pepper. Keep the poutine sauce warm on the stove until it is ready to use.

FOR THE SHEPHERD'S PIE

Preheat a large skillet to medium-high heat. Add the olive oil to the skillet along with the ground beef, breaking the meat up with a wooden spoon. Cook the meat until it is no longer pink, or for about 5 minutes. Add the mixed vegetables, salt and pepper. Sauté the veggies and beef for about 3 minutes. Stir in the Worcestershire sauce and the beef broth, and simmer for about 7 minutes. Using a slotted spoon, place the beef mixture into a bowl and set it aside. Cover and keep it warm until it is ready to use.

Preheat the oven to 350°F (177°C). In a large serving dish, spread the French fries into an even layer. Top the French fries with the shepherd's pie and the white cheddar cheese curds, and then pour the poutine over the top. Place the dish into the oven for about 10 minutes, or until the cheese has melted.

SEVEN-LAYER GREEK DIP GRILLED CHEESE SANDWICH

Where there's a potluck gathering, there's sure to be seven-layer dip. No argument from me, but can we get an update on this dish? Who's with me? Whenever I'm looking to put a new spin on tradition, I go Greek. In this many-layered case, that means hummus, Greek yogurt, cucumber, olives, tomatoes, feta and fresh herbs. And while we're at it, instead of piling the ingredients into a casserole dish, why not turn it into a full-fledged grilled cheese sandwich! Brilliant! Just layer those ingredients onto sourdough slices, and top with more cheese. You'll have everyone at the potluck saying "Opa!"

SERVES 4

12 slices sourdough bread, toasted

½ cup (123 g) plain hummus

½ cup (142 g) plain Greek yogurt

8 tomato slices

1 cup (113 g) shredded Monterrey jack cheese

1 cup (113 g) shredded mozzarella cheese

1 whole cucumber, sliced into rounds

1 cup (134 g) pitted and chopped kalamata olives

½ cup (105 g) diced red onion

¼ cup (42 g) crumbled feta cheese

¼ cup (5 g) chopped fresh parsley

Preheat a stove-top griddle to medium heat and spray it with non-stick cooking spray. While the griddle heats up, assemble your grilled cheese sandwich. You will need 3 slices of sourdough bread per sandwich.

First, spread 2 tablespoons (15 g) of hummus on top of the sourdough. Next, spread 2 tablespoons (17 g) of the Greek yogurt over the hummus. Top the Greek yogurt with two tomato slices, followed by ¼ cup (28 g) of Monterrey jack cheese and ¼ cup (28 g) of the shredded mozzarella. Next, take a slice of sourdough and place it on top of the cheese. Place about 4 to 5 cucumber rounds on top of the sourdough. Then top the cucumbers with ¼ cup (33 g) of chopped olives, ¼ cup (52 g) of diced onion, 1 tablespoon (10 g) of feta, 1 tablespoon (1 g) of parsley, ¼ cup (28 g) of Monterrey jack cheese, ¼ cup (28 g) of mozzarella and the remaining slice of sourdough. Phew!

Take the assembled sandwich and place it on the griddle. Press down on the top of the sandwich with a small skillet to make sure the cheese starts to melt. Flip the sandwich after about 4 minutes. Continue to cook the grilled cheese until it's golden brown and delicious. Repeat the process for the remaining four sandwiches!

Kitchen Tip: Toast the sourdough slices before you assemble the sandwich. This will keep the sourdough from becoming soggy as you build your epic seven-layer sandwich.

JAMBALAYA SPAGHETTI PIE

Rice is difficult to prepare perfectly. I either undercook it, overcook it or burn the crap out of it. Maybe rice and I just weren't meant to be? Which is a darn shame, because I love me some jambalaya. Jambalaya Spaghetti Pie is my way of enjoying Louisiana flavor, without the rice performance pressure. This twist on a much-loved comfort dish is particularly easy to make. Instead of mixing andouille sausage and veggies with rice, toss it with long strands of buttery spaghetti and bake until golden—just like pie. Failed pots of rice, no more!

SERVES 4

2 tbsp (28 g) clarified butter (page 183)

1 cup (150 g) chopped yellow onion

½ cup (12 g) chopped celery

1 cup (110 g) chopped red pepper

1 tsp kosher salt

1 tsp ground pepper

1 precooked andouille sausage link, about 6 oz (170 g), cut crosswise into 1-inch (2.5-cm) thick pieces

1 clove garlic, minced

1 tbsp (18 g) Cajun seasoning

2 (8-oz [460-g]) boneless, skinless chicken breasts, thinly-sliced

1 (14-oz [398-g]) can fire-roasted diced tomatoes

½ cup (121 ml) heavy whipping cream

2 cups (226 g) shredded mild cheddar cheese, divided

8 oz (227 g) dry spaghetti

2 large eggs, whisked

Fresh chopped parsley, for garnish

Preheat the oven to 425°F (218°C). Once the oven is heated, place a 3-quart (2.8 L) cast-iron skillet into the oven until ready to fill it with the jambalaya.

In a large Dutch oven preheated to medium-high heat, add the clarified butter. Add the onion, celery, red pepper, 1 teaspoon of the kosher salt and 1 teaspoon of the ground pepper. Sauté the veggies until they start to soften, or about 5 minutes. Add in the andouille sausage to the Dutch oven and begin to brown it which should take about 3 to 4 minutes. Next, add the garlic, Cajun seasoning and sliced chicken into the Dutch oven and continue to cook until the chicken is no longer pink, or for about 6 minutes. Pour in the diced tomatoes and let the mixture simmer for about 5 minutes. Stir in the heavy cream and 1 cup (113 g) of the cheddar cheese, and toss to combine. Turn off the heat and set the Dutch oven aside.

Meanwhile, bring a large stock pot full of water to a boil. Add the spaghetti to the pot along with a pinch of salt and cook for about 10 minutes or until al dente. Drain the spaghetti. In a large bowl, add some of the whisked eggs along with the drained spaghetti and toss together. By doing this, you are tempering the eggs to ensure you don't end up scrambling them. Once combined, add in the rest of the whisked eggs and toss. Next, add the jambalaya mixture to the spaghetti and 1 cup (113 g) of the cheddar cheese. Toss again, making sure everything is well-incorporated.

Remove the preheated cast-iron skillet from the oven with an oven mitt, and spray it with non-stick cooking spray just for some extra insurance that the pie won't stick! Add the jambalaya spaghetti mixture to the skillet and top it with the remaining 1 cup (113 g) of cheese. Place the skillet back into the oven and bake for about 20 minutes or until the top is golden brown. Garnish with fresh chopped parsley and serve!

Variation: Mix up the pasta in this dish with penne, elbow macaroni or rigatoni!

EASY CUBAN CAESAR SALAD

Down the street from our house is a small Cuban café called Café Buchi. Whenever Mr. B and I need to slow down a bit, we go there to linger over a hot cup of café con leche, a juicy Cubano and a plate of fried plantains. There's something about the deep orange, red and blue walls of the restaurant mixed with turn-of-the century reclaimed wood that sets the mood to "deep relax," and reminds us to savor every moment. This Easy Cuban Caesar Salad is meant to be a starter for that sit-here-all-day mindset. It's got all the fixings of the standard Caesar salad, but with fried plantains, fresh avocado, red onion and tomatoes. Hurry up and start relaxing!

SERVES 4

4 hearts of romaine lettuce, shredded

½ cup (105 g) sliced red onion

1 cup (149 g) halved grape tomatoes

1 avocado, diced

1 clove garlic, minced

¼ tsp kosher salt

¼ tsp ground pepper

1 large egg yolk

1 tbsp (15 ml) lemon juice

½ tsp Dijon mustard

1 tsp ground oregano

1 tsp ground cumin

¼ cup (60 ml) olive oil

3 tbsp (18 g) grated Parmesan

Vegetable oil, for frying

2 ripe plantains, peeled and sliced into 1-inch (2.5-cm) rounds

In a large bowl, toss together the romaine, red onion, grape tomatoes and avocado. Next, in a small mixing bowl add the minced garlic, kosher salt, ground pepper and egg yolk. Stir until the mixture is well combined. Gently add in the lemon juice, mustard, oregano and cumin. Continue to whisk, gradually adding in the olive oil. Whisk until the dressing is thick and glossy. Stir in the Parmesan cheese. Taste to make sure the seasoning is spot-on. Add more salt and pepper, if desired. Pour the dressing over the romaine, and toss the salad.

Meanwhile, add the oil to a large cast-iron skillet that has been preheated over medium-high heat, filling it to about 1-inch (2.5-cm) high. Add the plantain rounds to the skillet and fry the plantains for about 2 to 3 minutes per side. Remove the plantains from the skillet with a pair of tongs and set them on a plate lined with a paper towel. Repeat the process until all the plantains have been fried. Sprinkle the tops of the plantains with salt and let them cool completely before topping the romaine salad with them!

Kitchen Tip: When you are shopping for plantains at the grocery store, make sure you purchase ripe ones. They should be yellow in color and soft to the touch. Also, the easiest way to prepare a plantain is to cut the top and bottom off first. Then take a small knife and run the knife along the skin from the top to the bottom. Carefully peel away the skin and then slice.

CHICKEN CARBONARA-STUFFED EGG ROLLS

Ever get a hankering for certain combinations of food? Like Frosty's and French fries? Or Cheetos and ketchup? Hey—don't knock it 'til you try it—I swear it tastes like shrimp cocktail. These Chicken Carbonara Egg Rolls were born from a random craving I had one day. I hadn't had Italian or Chinese food in a while, and decided these two cuisines needed a proper introduction. And let me tell you, they became total besties in about two nano seconds. Silky and luxurious chicken carbonara stuffed inside a golden pouch of fried goodness—these egg rolls make for a killer appetizer or side.

YIELDS 12 EGG ROLLS

2 slices bacon, chopped

1 clove garlic, minced

¾ cup (170 ml) heavy whipping cream

¼ cup (20 g) grated Parmesan

2 large egg yolks

2 tbsp (8 g) chopped fresh basil

2 tbsp (8 g) chopped fresh parsley

¼ tsp kosher salt

¼ tsp ground pepper

2 cups (280 g) cooked ground chicken

1 tsp grated lemon zest

2 tbsp (18 g) all-purpose flour

2 tbsp (30 ml) water

12 (6-inch [15-cm]) egg roll wrappers

Vegetable oil, for frying

In a large skillet preheated to medium-high heat, add the bacon and the garlic. Sauté the bacon until it is cooked and crispy, or for about 4 minutes. Meanwhile, in a large bowl, combine the cream, Parmesan, egg yolks, basil, parsley, kosher salt and ground pepper. Turn the skillet with the bacon to medium-low heat. Add in the cream mixture along with the cooked chicken. Stir to combine. Keep stirring, making sure the eggs don't scramble. Cook for about 4 minutes, or until the mixture has thickened. Remove the skillet from the heat and stir in the lemon zest.

Next, combine the water and flour in a small bowl. Place one egg roll wrapper with a corner pointed toward you onto a work surface. Take about 1½ tablespoons (22 ml) of the chicken carbonara mixture and place the mixture in the center of the egg roll wrapper. Using your index finger, spread some of the water and flour mixture along the edge of the wrapper. Next, fold two of the corners together to make a triangle. Gently fold in the sides and then roll tightly, sealing the edges with the flour mixture. Repeat the process to make the additional egg rolls.

In a large Dutch oven, add the vegetable oil, filling to about 2 inches (5 cm) high. Using a frying thermometer, preheat the oil to 350°F (177°C). In batches, add the egg rolls and fry them until they are golden brown on all sides, about 4 minutes. Remove them with tongs and allow them to cool slightly before eating!

Kitchen Tip: If you are making these egg rolls for a party, you can assemble the rolls ahead of time. Keep the rolls in an airtight container in the fridge and then pull the egg rolls out and fry them as needed before guests arrive!

REUBEN ROLLS *with* BUTTERED RYE BREADCRUMBS

A piece of true-love trivia: Mr. B is largely responsible for the growth of my palate. I'd follow that man and his taste for good food to the ends of the earth (and now that I think about it, I have literally done just that). In honor of my sweetie's priceless contribution, I'm putting Mr. B's favorite sandwich in the spotlight: presenting Reuben Rolls with Buttered Rye Breadcrumbs. Now, you may be thinking, hey, this "sandwich" is rather . . . roll-like. True, true. But this dish is no phony: all the fixings of a top-rate reuben are nestled inside the puff pastry—corned beef, pastrami, sauerkraut, Swiss cheese and thousand island dressing. Top with some buttered rye breadcrumbs, and be thankful that Mr. B picked me. I know I am.

SERVES 4 TO 6

2 sheets puff pastry, thawed

6 oz (186 g) thinly sliced corned beef, divided

4 oz (112 g) thinly sliced pastrami, divided

1 cup (150 g) sauerkraut, divided

1 cup (100 g) Swiss cheese, divided

¼ cup (60 ml) thousand island dressing, divided

1 egg, whisked

2 slices (56 g) day-old rye bread, crusts removed

2 tbsp (28 g) unsalted melted butter

Pinch of salt and pepper

Preheat the oven to 350°F (177°C). Spray two baking sheets with non-stick cooking spray and set them aside.

Next, lay the puff pastry sheet on a work surface sprinkled lightly with flour. Take each pastry sheet and cut it in half, creating 2 large rectangles. You will have 4 total. On a rectangle, lay 2 ounces (56 g) of corned beef and 1 ounce (28 g) of pastrami. Top the meat with ¼ cup (38 g) of sauerkraut, ¼ cup (25 g) of Swiss cheese and 1 tablespoon (15 ml) of thousand island dressing. Take a pastry brush and brush the edges of the rectangle with the egg. Starting with the long end, roll up the reuben mixture, finishing with the seam-side down. Place the roll on a baking sheet and repeat the process until all the reuben rolls have been assembled.

Once the rolls have been assembled, place them into the fridge for about 15 minutes to set. Meanwhile, make the buttered rye breadcrumbs. Place 2 to 3 slices of rye bread on a baking sheet. Toast the bread for about 5 to 7 minutes. Remove the bread from the oven and place it into a small food processor. Pulse the bread a few times and then add the melted butter, a pinch of salt and a pinch of pepper. Once combined, set the breadcrumbs aside in a small bowl.

Next, remove the rolls from the fridge and, using a pastry brush, brush the tops of the rolls with the egg and sprinkle them with buttered rye breadcrumbs. Place the baking sheets into the oven and bake the rolls for about 25 minutes, or until golden brown. Slice the long rolls into four miniature rolls.

Variation: Upgrade your next soup and sandwich gig by making a variety of rolls. Fill the puff pastry with ham and Swiss, or roast beef and cheddar! Go crazy!

GOULASH-STUFFED BELL PEPPERS

Goulash is a traditional Hungarian stew made of vegetables and meat and seasoned with lots of paprika. Truth? Whenever I hear the word "goulash," I don't think of a stew. I actually hear and see the word "ghoulish," which is neither here, nor there. Anyway, I remember eating ghoulish—I mean goulash—a handful of times as a kid and loving it. The simple, hearty sauce of tomatoes mixed with lots of veggies, ground beef and elbow pasta (my fav!) made for a fun dish to dive into. Instead of taking a stew form, my goulash is stuffed inside delicious bell peppers! Baked until golden and delicious, these peppers are positively stuffed with comfort.

SERVES 4

4 large bell peppers

1 tbsp (15 ml) olive oil

1 lb (450 g) lean ground beef

1 cup (150 g) chopped yellow onion

1 tsp garlic powder

1 tsp kosher salt

1 tsp ground pepper

½ cup (120 ml) beef broth

½ cup (120 ml) red wine

1 (15-oz [425-g]) can diced, fire-roasted tomatoes

1 (15-oz [425-g]) can tomato sauce

1 tbsp (16 g) tomato paste

2 tbsp (16 g) ground paprika

1 bay leaf

1 tsp caraway seeds

6 tbsp (90 ml) green olive juice

1 cup (134 g) diced green olives

1 cup (100 g) uncooked elbow macaroni

1 cup (113 g) shredded mozzarella cheese

1 cup (113 g) shredded Parmesan

Fresh chopped parsley, for garnish

Preheat the oven to 350°F (177°C). Slice the tops off the peppers and scrape out the ribs and seeds. Spray a 9 x 9-inch (23 x 23-cm) baking dish with non-stick cooking spray and place the peppers into it cut-side up. Set the dish aside.

In a large Dutch oven preheated to medium-high heat, add the olive oil and the ground beef. Using a wooden spoon to break up the meat, cook the beef for about 5 to 6 minutes or until it is no longer pink. If there is excess fat in the bottom of the Dutch oven simply spoon it out. You want to have about a tablespoon (15 g) of fat in the Dutch oven.

Next, add the yellow onion, garlic powder, kosher salt and pepper. Sauté the onions with the beef until they are softened, or for about 3 to 4 minutes. Stir in the beef broth, red wine, fire-roasted tomatoes, tomato sauce, tomato paste, paprika, bay leaf, caraway seeds, olive juice and green olives. Bring the mixture to a boil and then reduce it to a simmer and cook for about 10 minutes. Next, stir in the macaroni and cover the Dutch oven. Simmer for another 10 minutes or until the pasta is tender, stirring occasionally to make sure the macaroni doesn't stick to the bottom of the oven. Turn off the heat and discard the bay leaf.

Using a slotting spoon, take some of the goulash mixture and fill the peppers to the top. Next, top each pepper with one-quarter of the mozzarella and one-quarter of the Parmesan. In the bottom of the baking dish pour a small amount of water. This will help the peppers to steam and make them tender to eat. Cover the baking dish with foil and bake the peppers for about 30 minutes. Then remove the foil and bake for another 10 minutes until the cheese is lightly browned. Garnish the tops with chopped parsley. Mmmm!

Variation: If you prefer a little spice in this dish, add 1 chipotle pepper to the sauce.

Kitchen Tip: Goulash is a great dish to add to your meal prep for the week. It tastes better the longer it sits. Simply make the goulash on Sunday, then on Wednesday stuff the peppers and bake the dish off for a quick and delicious meal!

CHICKEN CORDON BLEU EMPANADAS

Sometimes I feel like a food matchmaker. A dish will "sing" to me, wanting me to find a new mate, just like the father in "Fiddler on the Roof," looking for a match for his daughter. Well, I heard the cry of chicken cordon bleu. This traditional Swiss dish was tired of being wrapped in a ham slice and then deep fried. So, I decided to introduce the famous chicken dish to the one and only Argentinean empanada. A stuffed hand-pie that is baked to a golden perfection. These two were made for each other! Take the cheesy filling of a chicken cordon bleu and nestle it into a soft dough, gently wrap the edges and then bake into marital bliss. Cue the music: "Matchmaker, matchmaker, make me a match . . . "

YIELDS 7 EMPANADAS

EMPANADA DOUGH

2¼ cups (315 g) all-purpose flour

1½ tsp (9 g) kosher salt

½ cup (112 g) unsalted butter, cold, chopped into cubes

¼ cup (60 ml) cold water

2 large eggs, divided

CHICKEN CORDON BLEU

2 tbsp (28 g) unsalted butter

1 shallot, minced

2 cloves garlic, minced

⅓ cup (37 g) shredded parmesan

¾ cup (180 ml) heavy cream

1 tsp Dijon mustard

1¼ cups (155 g) diced rotisserie chicken

3 to 4 prosciutto slices, cut into small pieces

1 cup (113 g) shredded Swiss cheese

Kitchen Tip: Treat the flour mixture with tender care! You don't want to overwork the dough when it's in the food processor or while kneading it because if you do, the dough won't be as flaky.

FOR THE EMPANADA DOUGH

In a large food processor, add the flour and kosher salt. Pulse a few times. Next, add in the unsalted butter cubes. Pulse again for a few times. In a small bowl, whisk together 1 large egg and the cold water. Next, stream in the egg mixture and continue to pulse until the dough resembles pea-size crumbs. Remove the empanada dough from the food processor and place it on a work surface that is dusted with flour. Gently press the dough until the dough comes together adding a little bit more water if the dough is still crumbly. Shape the dough into a large flat disc, cover it with plastic wrap and place the disc into the fridge for at least an hour.

FOR THE CHICKEN CORDON BLEU

While the dough rests, prep the chicken cordon bleu filling. In a large skillet preheated to medium-high heat melt the unsalted butter. Add in the shallot and the garlic. Sauté the veggies until they are softened, or for about 3 minutes. Next, add in the Parmesan cheese, cream, Dijon mustard and chicken. Continue to stir until the mixture thickens, which should take about 3 minutes. Once thickened, remove the skillet from the heat and add the salt and the pepper, if needed. Set the skillet aside.

TO ASSEMBLE

Preheat the oven to 400°F (204°C). Once the dough has chilled, remove it from the fridge and place it back on the work surface that is lightly dusted with flour. Let the dough sit out for about 15 to 20 minutes so it's easier to roll out. Roll the dough out into a thin layer about ⅛-inch (0.3-cm) thick. Using a 5-inch (13-cm) biscuit cutter, cut out 7 circles of the dough. Place the circles on a baking sheet that is lined with parchment paper.

Next, take about 1½ tablespoons (22 ml) of the cordon bleu filling and place it in the middle of a dough circle. Top the filling with a small piece of prosciutto and some of the shredded Swiss cheese. Repeat until all the circles have been filled. Whisk the remaining egg in a small bowl. Using a pastry brush, brush the edges of the dough circle with the egg wash. Fold the empanada circle in half pressing with your fingers and using a fork to help seal the edges. Brush the top of the empanada with more egg wash. Repeat these steps until all the empanadas have been assembled.

Place the baking sheet in the oven and bake the empanadas for about 25 to 35 minutes, or until they turn golden brown. Serve warm and enjoy!

BEEF STROGANOFF FRENCH BREAD TOASTS

Beef stroganoff has been around since the nineteenth century. Can you believe it? That means folks have been jonesing for this Russian dish for over 150 years. I totally get why this comfort food is such a survivor—mushrooms sautéed and mixed with ground beef, paprika and sour cream, until a rich luxurious sauce forms and is dolloped over buttered noodles—sounds pretty good, right? Since we're talking mash-ups, this recipe takes the base of the stroganoff, and instead of topping noodles with it, why not smother the top of a French loaf with it? These Beef Stroganoff French Bread Toasts are super fun to make and are a great option for dinner on the fly, or fancy enough to serve as a handheld appetizer!

SERVES 4 TO 6

1 loaf of French bread, sliced in half

1 tbsp (15 ml) olive oil

1¼ cups (95 g) cremini mushrooms

1 tsp kosher salt, divided

1 tsp ground pepper, divided

3 tbsp (42 g) unsalted butter

1 cup (150 g) diced yellow onion

1 clove garlic, minced

1 lb (450 g) lean ground beef

3 tbsp (27 g) all-purpose flour

2 tsp (4 g) ground paprika

1½ cups (360 ml) beef broth

1 tsp Dijon mustard

½ cup (60 g) sour cream

2 cups (226 g) shredded havarti cheese

Fresh chopped parsley, for garnish

Variation: Want to keep this dish on the lighter side? Try subbing the beef for chicken and adding Greek yogurt instead of sour cream.

Preheat the oven to 400°F (204°C). Line a baking sheet with foil and spray with non-stick cooking spray and set aside. Place the French loaf halves on the baking sheet and scoop out some of the extra bread, leaving room to nestle the beef stroganoff. Set the baking sheet aside.

In a large Dutch oven preheated to medium-high heat, add the olive oil and mushrooms. Sauté the mushrooms until slightly golden brown, about 3 minutes, and then add ½ teaspoon of kosher salt and ½ teaspoon of pepper. Keep sautéing the mushrooms until they are golden brown, another few minutes. Using a slotted spoon, remove the mushrooms from the Dutch oven and place them into a mixing bowl. Set the mushrooms aside.

Turn the heat to medium and melt the butter in the Dutch oven. Once the butter has melted, add the onion, garlic, ½ teaspoon of kosher salt, and ½ teaspoon of ground pepper. Sauté the veggies until they are softened, or for about 3 to 4 minutes. Next, add the ground beef and, using a wooden spoon to break up the meat, cook the beef until it is no longer pink, or for about 5 minutes. Add the cooked mushrooms back in and stir to thoroughly combine.

Add the flour and paprika to the ground beef and begin to stir until the flour has been cooked out, or about 1 or 2 minutes. Next, pour in the beef stock and stir to make sure everything is well combined. Bring the ingredients in the Dutch oven to a boil and then lower to a simmer. Simmer the mixture for about 10 minutes and then remove the Dutch oven from the heat. Stir in the Dijon mustard and the sour cream.

Next, divide the beef stroganoff mixture between the two loaf halves. Top each half with 1 cup (113 g) of the havarti cheese. Place the baking sheet into the oven and bake the loaves for about 15 minutes or until the cheese is golden and bubbly. Remove the baking sheet from the oven and let the loaves cool for a few minutes. Once you are able to handle them, cut the loaves into square-sized toasts and garnish the tops with parsley and watch the toasts disappear!

Vintage Classics Re-Mixed

Growing up in the Midwest, three square meals a day were part of our daily routine. Yes, it was predictable, but life was simple growing up on the southern plains of Kansas. Each of our meals was set aside for casual conversation and enjoyment, with dinner being the most important meal for my immediate family.

Every evening, my parents made sure to sit my brothers and me down at our oval, wooden dining table to eat a hot meal and discuss the trials and tribulations of the day. I remember dragging my feet to the table thinking to my nine-year-old self, "I'm not even hungry. I bet if I eat fast I won't miss tonight's episode of *Blossom* or *Full House*."

As my parents went around the table asking my brothers and me how our day went, I would forget about the *Full House* episode I desperately wanted to watch. My younger brother, Jordan, an ever-so-funny guy, would spout off a funny joke or mimic a celebrity, which would bring the whole table to stomach-aching laughter. Sometimes an hour could pass and we'd still be at the table.

Thankfully my mother made hearty vintage classics like chicken parmesan, fish sticks or company pot roast. All these dishes were meant to hold up for lengthy dinners. In between laughter, fights or neighborhood gossip, classic comfort food dishes like these hold their own at the dinner table.

This chapter is made to take those classic vintage recipes and modernize them with a new ingredient or flavor or two. From Slow Cooker Company Pot Roast Noodle Bowls (page 102) to Chicken Parmesan-Stuffed Crêpes (page 116), and Beef Wellington-Stuffed Squashes (page 124) to Shrimp Scampi Zucchini Noodle Bake (page 113), you'll love these old favorites made new for your lovable crew!

SLOW COOKER COMPANY POT ROAST NOODLE BOWLS

A comfort food cookbook without a recipe for pot roast? Not on my watch, friends. Whether it's braised in a Dutch oven or simmered in a slow cooker, pot roast is still the king of comfort. I'm mixing it up here by serving pot roast via noodle bowls—instant update! These bowls have all the flavors of a traditional company pot roast, with noodles and a seven-minute egg added for good measure. If you've got a dinner party on the horizon, now's the time to grab a bookmark . . .

SERVES 4

2 tbsp (30 ml) olive oil

2 tsp (12 g) kosher salt, divided

2 tsp (12 g) ground pepper, divided

2½ lb (1.13 kg) boneless beef chuck roast

1 cup (150 g) chopped yellow onion

1 cup (128 g) peeled and chopped carrots

1 cup (101 g) chopped celery

3 cloves garlic, minced

1 russet potato, peeled and chopped

1 (14-oz [411-g]) can whole stewed tomatoes

1 cup (237 ml) red wine

1 cup (237 ml) beef broth

1 bay leaf

2 sprigs fresh rosemary

3 sprigs fresh thyme

4 large eggs

Ramen noodles, cooked, discard seasoning packet

In a large skillet preheated to medium-high heat, add the olive oil. Sprinkle 1 teaspoon of kosher salt and 1 teaspoon of ground pepper on one side of the pot roast. Add the seasoned side of the pot roast to the skillet. Sprinkle the other side with 1 teaspoon of kosher salt and 1 teaspoon of ground pepper. Sear the pot roast for about 4 minutes on the first side and then flip and continue to sear on the second side for about 2 to 3 minutes. If you need to add extra olive oil to the skillet, that's okay! Once the pot roast has been seared, remove the skillet from the heat and set it aside.

Next, add the onion, carrots, celery, garlic and potatoes to the bottom of a slow cooker. Place the seared beef on top of the veggies, followed by the tomatoes. In the skillet you used to sear the pot roast, return it back to medium-high heat and add the red wine. You want to deglaze the skillet, scraping up all of those brown bits. Once you've deglazed the skillet, pour the wine into the slow cooker followed by the beef broth. Place the bay leaf, rosemary and thyme on top of the roast. Cover the slow cooker and cook, low and slow, for 8 hours.

About 30 minutes before the pot roast is done cooking, make the seven-minute eggs. To make the eggs, fill a stock pot with water and bring it to a boil. Gently add the eggs to the water and set a timer for 7 minutes. Once the timer goes off, move the eggs to an ice bath to cool completely. Once cooled, crack each egg slightly and remove the shell. Slice the egg in half when you are ready to serve.

Once the pot roast is done, remove the bay leaf, rosemary, thyme and discard them. Next, remove the roast from the slow cooker with a pair of tongs and place it on a cutting board. Shred the pot roast using two forks. Using a fine strainer, strain the broth to remove the solids. You should have two bowls—one for the veggies and one for the broth. Divide the Ramen noodles among four bowls. Ladle some of the broth into each bowl. Top each bowl with veggies and shredded pot roast. Add one seven-minute egg to each bowl and let the slurping begin!

Variation: You can certainly substitute the beef with chicken or pork! For a vegetarian option, slow cook all the vegetables in a broth and then stir in tofu.

Kitchen Tip: Pull the chuck roast from the fridge an hour before cooking to allow it to come to room temperature. This will ensure that the roast cooks evenly.

VEGETARIAN OSSO BUCO *with* GOUDA POLENTA

During the winter months, I crave hearty comfort food. Don't we all? It's only natural as we enter hibernation mode. Nothing beats a bowl of hot soup or stew as you sit by the fire and watch the snow fall gently from the sky. Well, what if I told you I could beat that scenario? GASP! Vegetarian Osso Buco with Gouda Polenta just might do it. This dish is a healthier version of the traditional osso buco made with veal shanks. Seared carrots act as the hearty star, while sautéed mushrooms, onions, celery and red wine give this dish a depth of flavor found only in slow-cooked meals. Pour it over some smoked gouda polenta and you've got yourself a health-conscious comfort experience.

SERVES 4

2 tbsp (28 g) clarified butter (page 183)

6 large carrots, cut into thirds

2¼ tsp (17 g) kosher salt, divided

2 tsp (9 g) ground pepper, divided

1 cup (70 g) roughly chopped baby bella mushrooms

1 cup (85 g) roughly chopped shitake mushrooms, stems discarded

2 cloves garlic, minced

½ cup (75 g) chopped yellow onion

½ cup (51 g) chopped celery

1 tbsp (16 g) tomato paste

1 cup (240 ml) dry red wine

2 cups (480 ml) vegetable or mushroom stock

1 fresh rosemary sprig

1 fresh thyme sprig

1 bay leaf

3 cups (720 ml) water

1 cup (175 g) instant polenta

1½ cups (170 g) shredded gouda cheese

1 tbsp (14 g) unsalted butter

¼ cup (60 ml) heavy cream

Fresh chopped parsley, for garnish

In a large Dutch oven preheated to medium-high heat, add the clarified butter, carrots, 1 teaspoon of kosher salt and 1 teaspoon of ground pepper. Brown the carrots for a few minutes on each side. Remove the carrots from the skillet and place them into a bowl. Set the bowl aside.

In the same skillet, add the chopped mushrooms. Sauté the mushrooms until they are slightly golden brown, or for about 3 minutes. Next, add in the garlic, onions, celery, ½ teaspoon of salt and ½ teaspoon of ground pepper. Sauté the veggies until they are softened, or for about 5 minutes. Next, add the tomato paste and stir to combine. Add the carrots back into the skillet along with the red wine. Make sure you scrape up all that yummy goodness on the bottom of the pan. Let the liquid reduce a little, or for about 4 minutes. Next, add in the mushroom stock, rosemary sprig, thyme sprig and bay leaf. Bring the mixture to a boil and then reduce it to a simmer over low heat. Cover the Dutch oven and cook it for about an hour, stirring occasionally to keep the vegetables from burning.

While the osso buco cooks, prepare the polenta. In a large saucepan, bring the water to a simmer. Pour in the polenta and begin to whisk it. Simmer until polenta begins to thicken, about 5 to 7 minutes. Stir in the cheese, butter, cream, ¾ teaspoon of salt and ½ teaspoon of pepper. Set this mixture aside.

To serve, remove the rosemary sprig, thyme sprig and bay leaf from the Dutch oven. Divide the polenta among four bowls. Ladle the carrot and mushroom osso buco over the gouda polenta. Garnish with fresh parsley.

Variation: Swap out baby bella mushrooms for high-end morels when they are in season. Morels will add some sass when you serve this dish at your next dinner party!

TURMERIC TUNA MELT SKILLET

My little brother Jordan is a huge fan of the tuna melt (or any sandwich that calls for canned tuna, really). But I've always trusted my nose, so I'd never quite understood the appeal. But one fine day at the quickie sub shop, he convinced me to give tuna a chance. Fearing it would taste something like a dirty sock, I sunk my teeth into the overstuffed sub, and melted. I gave my bro the thumbs up—yep, this sub is legit. Nowadays, when I get a hankering for that "legit" level of tuna experience, this skillet is my solution. Mix a day-old baguette with the usual tuna melt ingredients, and add turmeric. Turmeric and tuna were made for each other—scout's honor. Put everything into the skillet and bake. What you get is a giant helping of the best tuna sandwich ever!

SERVES 4

5 cups (553 g) baguette cubes, cut into 1-inch (2.5-cm) pieces

1 cup (200 g) canned tuna in water, drained

⅓ cup (77 g) mayonnaise

1½ tsp (16 g) turmeric powder

1 tsp ground cumin

2 tbsp (10 g) chopped red onion

1 tbsp (15 ml) lemon juice

1 clove garlic, minced

2 tbsp (24 g) chopped parsley

½ cup (57 g) shredded mozzarella cheese

½ cup (57 g) shredded mild cheddar cheese

1 tsp kosher salt

1 tsp ground pepper

Preheat the oven to 375°F (191°C).

In a large bowl, combine the baguette cubes, tuna, mayonnaise, turmeric, cumin, red onion, lemon juice, garlic, parsley, mozzarella, cheddar, kosher salt and pepper. If the mixture looks too dry, add some olive to the bowl and keep mixing.

Once everything is combined, pour the tuna mixture into 10-inch (25-cm) cast-iron skillet. Top the mixture with extra cheese and bake until it is warmed through and golden brown on top, about 12 to 15 minutes. Careful to use oven mitts, remove the skillet from the oven and serve.

Variation: Don't have canned tuna on hand? Cooked salmon would be a great alternative!

TURKEY TACO PIZZA *with* CAULIFLOWER CRUST

Growing up, Saturday night was pizza delivery night. Believe it or not, at some point our family held the record for the most deliveries in the neighborhood (the pizza place actually kept track—nice!). We always had a standard cheese pizza at the table, but every now and then a taco pizza would make an appearance. Refried beans, ground beef, tomatoes, taco chips and cheese piled high on a golden crust . . . it was a slice of heaven. Fast-forward a few decades and this girl still craves taco pizza, but I figure it could use a refresh. The result is Turkey Taco Pizza with Cauliflower Crust. Taco-flavored ground turkey still satisfies the craving, while the cauliflower crust keeps things light. Trust me, this will become a Saturday night staple in your house, too!

SERVES 2 TO 3

1 lb (450 g) cauliflower, cut into florets

¼ cup (28 g) shredded mozzarella cheese

¼ cup (28 g) shredded pepper jack cheese

½ tsp dried oregano

1½ tsp (4 g) garlic powder, divided

½ tsp red pepper flakes

¾ tsp kosher salt, divided

1 tbsp (8 g) cornmeal

1 large egg

½ lb (230 g) ground turkey

1 tbsp (8 g) ground chili powder

1 tsp ground cumin

1 tsp ground coriander

1 tsp ground paprika

½ tsp ground pepper

1 tbsp (15 ml) olive oil

½ cup (120 ml) tomato sauce

1 cup (113 g) shredded Monterey jack cheese

Shredded lettuce, for garnish

Diced fresh tomato, for garnish

Diced red onion, for garnish

Sour cream, for garnish

Fresh chopped cilantro, for garnish

Preheat the oven to 450°F (232°C).

Lay a silicone liner or a sheet of parchment paper on a baking sheet. In a food processor, add the cauliflower florets. Pulse a few times until the cauliflower is about the size of peas. Remove the cauliflower mixture from the food processor and place it into a microwave-safe bowl. Cook the cauliflower on high for 2 minutes. Remove the cauliflower from the microwave and let it cool.

Place the cooled cauliflower in a dish towel and twist it tightly a couple of times to remove the moisture. Place the cauliflower in a bowl and add the mozzarella, pepper jack cheese, oregano, ½ teaspoon of garlic powder, red pepper flakes, ¼ teaspoon of kosher salt and the cornmeal. Gently combine everything with your fingers. Add the egg and finish combining. Form the cauliflower into a ball. Place the cauliflower ball on the baking sheet and use your fingers to form a 10- to 11-inch (25- to 28-cm) diameter crust that is about ¼-inch (0.6-cm) thick. Place the cauliflower crust into the oven and bake it for about 10 to 12 minutes. You want it crispy, but not burnt.

Meanwhile, in a large bowl combine the ground turkey, chili powder, 1 teaspoon of cumin, coriander, paprika, 1 teaspoon of garlic powder, ½ teaspoon of kosher salt and ground pepper. Preheat a skillet to medium-high heat and add the olive oil along with the ground turkey. Sauté the turkey for about 4 to 5 minutes, or until it is no longer pink. Remove the skillet from the heat and set it aside.

Once the cauliflower crust has been partially baked, remove it from the oven. Spread the tomato sauce on top of the cauliflower crust leaving a ½-inch (1.3-cm) border. Top the tomato sauce with the ground turkey and Monterey jack cheese. Place the pizza back into the oven for an additional 10 to 12 minutes, or until the cheese is nice and golden brown. Remove the pizza from the oven and let it rest for 5 minutes. Before slicing, top the pizza with shredded lettuce, tomatoes, red onion, sour cream and cilantro!

FRIED POLENTA "STEAKS" *with* MUSHROOM GRAVY

Raise your hand if you like chicken-fried steak. It's the ultimate comfort food in my opinion, and I admit to secretly ordering this dish when no one is looking. (You can put your hand down, now.) Chicken-fried steak with gravy was a meal for superheroes back in the day, right? You'd need a hearty meal to fight crime . . . or your 9-to-5 boss. Fast forward a half a century later and chicken-fried steak is now reserved for those 2 a.m. diner outings. It's something I plunge into on a semi-annual basis, but I always feel like two miles of bad road the day after. And the day after that. So rather than risk feeling like asphalt, here's a healthier take. Polenta is a great vegetarian substitute that acts like steak in this new version—just sear it and top it with mushroom gravy. Now we can feel good about eating this comforting dish at 5 p.m. with a glass of pinot noir.

SERVES 4

MUSHROOM GRAVY

1 tbsp (15 ml) olive oil

2 cups (150 g) sliced baby bella mushrooms

½ cup (75 g) julienned red onion

1½ tsp (4 g) chopped fresh rosemary

¼ tsp kosher salt

¼ tsp ground pepper

2 tbsp (28 g) unsalted butter

2 tbsp (16 g) all-purpose flour

1 cup (237 ml) chicken or vegetable stock

POLENTA STEAKS

3 cups (705 ml) water

1 cup (170 g) instant polenta or quick cooking grits

1 cup (113 g) shredded mozzarella cheese

2 tbsp (28 g) unsalted butter, divided

¼ cup (60 ml) heavy cream

¼ tsp kosher salt

¼ tsp ground pepper

Fresh chopped parsley, for garnish

FOR THE MUSHROOM GRAVY

In a skillet preheated to medium heat, add the olive oil and mushrooms. Sauté the mushrooms until golden brown, or about 5 minutes. Next, add the red onion, rosemary, kosher salt and ground pepper. Continue to sauté the veggies until softened, or for about 4 minutes. Add the butter to the skillet and let it melt. Add the flour and whisk for about a minute or until all the veggies are coated with the flour. Gradually whisk in the chicken or vegetable stock. Continue whisking until the gravy has thickened, about 3 to 4 minutes. Taste and adjust the seasonings if needed and then remove the skillet from the heat.

FOR THE POLENTA STEAKS

Spray a 9 x 9-inch (23 x 23-cm) baking dish with non-stick cooking spray and set it aside. In a large saucepan, bring the water to a simmer. Pour in the polenta and begin to whisk it. Simmer until the polenta begins to thicken, or about 3 to 5 minutes. Stir in the cheese, 1 tablespoon (14 g) of the butter, the cream, salt and pepper. Remove the saucepan from the heat and pour the polenta into the prepared baking dish. Gently press the polenta evenly into the baking dish. Cover the baking dish with plastic wrap and let it chill for at least 3 hours in the fridge. Once chilled, cut the polenta into four 4-inch (10-cm) squares. Preheat a skillet to medium-high heat. Melt 1 tablespoon (14 g) of butter and sear each side of the polenta until it is golden brown. Remove the polenta from the skillet and place it on a serving plate. Top it with warm mushroom gravy, sprinkle with parsley and serve!

Variation: If you want to mix things up, try adding different spices like oregano, thyme or herbs de provence to the polenta steaks. Think of the steaks as a blank canvas to which you can add whatever flavors fits your theme for the evening. Try adding Latin or Indian spices to kick things up a notch!

SHRIMP SCAMPI ZUCCHINI NOODLE BAKE

Vegetable noodles. Are these not the greatest thing since sliced bread? For years, I've been cutting pasta from our weekly dinner routine, because it's simply too tempting to over-consume. I adore carbs in every way possible, but I always feel like the Stay Puft Marshmallow Man from the movie *Ghostbusters*, after consuming a giant bowl. Thankfully, the universe has gifted us with vegetable noodles, so pasta dishes like Shrimp Scampi can make their way back to menus once again. This is one of my favorite dishes because it's light, flavorful, super easy to make and can feed a crowd in a hurry!

SERVES 4

6 tbsp (84 g) unsalted butter, divided

4 tbsp (60 ml) olive oil, divided

½ cup (50 g) diced shallot

¾ tsp kosher salt, divided

¾ tsp ground pepper, divided

3 cloves garlic, minced

1 lb (450 g) shrimp, peeled, deveined

½ cup (118 ml) white wine

2 tbsp (30 ml) fresh lemon juice

½ tsp lemon pepper, divided

⅓ cup (20 g) chopped parsley

1 cup (50 g) panko

6 cups (900 g) zucchini noodles, about 2 medium zucchini (page 183)

Preheat the oven to 400°F (204°C).

In a large skillet, melt 2 tablespoons (28 g) of the butter over medium-high heat. Add 2 tablespoons (30 ml) of olive oil, the shallot, ¼ teaspoon of salt and ¼ teaspoon of pepper. Sauté until the shallots have softened, or about 3 minutes. Add the garlic and sauté for 30 seconds. Meanwhile, season the shrimp with ½ teaspoon of kosher salt and ½ teaspoon of ground pepper. Add the shrimp to the skillet and cook for about 1 minute per side. Remove the shrimp from the skillet and set it aside. In the same skillet, add the wine and the lemon juice. Bring the skillet to a slight simmer. Add the remaining 2 tablespoons (28 g) of butter, 2 tablespoons (30 ml) of olive oil and ¼ teaspoon of lemon pepper to the skillet. Once the butter has melted, add the shrimp back to the skillet. Remove the skillet from the heat and toss the shrimp with parsley.

In a small skillet, melt 2 tablespoons (28 g) of butter. Add the panko and remaining ¼ teaspoon of lemon pepper and stir to combine. Remove the skillet from the heat and set it aside to cool slightly.

Spray a 13 x 9-inch (33 x 23-cm) baking dish with non-stick cooking spray. In a large bowl, add the zucchini noodles. Pour in the shrimp scampi mixture into the bowl and gently toss. Pour the mixture into the prepared baking dish. Top the shrimp and noodle mixture with the lemon pepper panko. Bake the dish for about 15 minutes or until the panko is golden brown on top. Remove the dish from the oven and serve immediately.

Kitchen Tip: If you have a spiralizer, use the fettuccini-style blade. If you use a thicker cut, you will need to adjust the cooking time.

SOUTHERN SHRIMP QUINOA SALAD

The South knows how to feed your soul. If I lived below the Mason–Dixon line, I'd have a mandatory food pub crawl every day, just so I could eat she-crab soup, gobs of pimento cheese, fried chicken and red beans and rice. But even after sampling every Southern comfort food delight, I always find myself needing a reset. This Southern Shrimp Quinoa Salad is my way of satisfying those Southern cravings, while leaving some room in the waistline. Perfectly sautéed Cajun shrimp is tossed together with light, fluffy quinoa, along with olives, peppers and a squeeze of lemon on top—you're halfway to Dixie!

SERVES 4

1 cup (170 g) raw quinoa, rinsed three times

1½ cups (360 ml) chicken stock

1 tsp kosher salt, divided

¼ cup (26 g) jarred muffaletta salad

20 medium-size, raw shrimp, peeled and deveined

1 tbsp (8 g) Cajun seasoning

2 tbsp (28 g) clarified butter (page 183)

2 tbsp (30 ml) lemon juice

Fresh chopped parsley, for garnish

Lemon wedges, for garnish

In a large saucepan with a lid, add the quinoa, chicken stock and ½ teaspoon of the kosher salt and bring to a boil over medium-high heat. Reduce the heat to low, cover and simmer the quinoa for about 12 to 15 minutes or until the water has been absorbed. Remove the saucepan from the heat and set it aside to cool slightly, then transfer the quinoa to a large bowl. Toss in the muffaletta, stir to combine and set aside.

In a large bowl, combine the shrimp, Cajun seasoning and remaining ½ teaspoon of kosher salt. Toss all the ingredients together making sure everything is well combined. Preheat a large skillet to medium-high heat. Add the clarified butter followed by half of the shrimp. Sauté the shrimp for about 1 minute on the first side, flip, and continue to cook on the other side for about a minute. Remove the shrimp from the skillet and set them aside on a plate. Squeeze lemon juice over the tops of the shrimp. Repeat the process with the remaining shrimp.

To serve, divide the quinoa salad among four bowls. Place 5 shrimp into each bowl. Garnish the bowls with fresh parsley and a little squirt of lemon juice.

Kitchen Tip: Check out the label on your Cajun seasoning. If salt is the first ingredient, your shrimp will suffer, and I mean suffer from too much salt! Use either no-salt Cajun seasoning or one that has salt listed toward the end of the ingredient list.

CHICKEN PARMESAN–STUFFED CRÊPES

One of the first Christmas gifts I got Mr. B when we were dating was a French cookbook, along with a crêpe pan. Many guys would deem such a gift a threat to their manliness. But we had just been to Europe, and seeing as he showed great culinary potential, this was the gift I chose. He thanked me of course, but the cookbook and crêpe pan didn't appear again until we got married—after all, a crêpe pan isn't something the average American uses on a day-to-day basis. Once he began to use it, though, we found out how flexible it really is. This Chicken Parmesan–Stuffed Crêpe is the result of crepe pan experimentation, and I will state for the record that this recipe received a high-five from Mr. B. What's bad about crispy chicken smothered in marinara sauce and cheese, then baked? Absolutely nothing. This dish is great to serve on any occasion, because other than waiting for the crêpe batter to set, it comes together lickety-split. Now go break out that dusty crêpe pan!

SERVES 4

CREPES

1 cup (140 g) all-purpose flour

¼ teaspoon kosher salt

1½ cups (365 ml) whole milk

3 eggs

2 tbsp (28 g) unsalted butter, melted and cooled

1 tbsp (5 g) finely grated Parmesan cheese

1 tsp Italian seasoning

1 tbsp (15 ml) vegetable oil

CHICKEN PARMESAN

4 (4-oz [440-g]) boneless, skinless chicken breasts

2 tsp (4 g) ground oregano, divided

2 tsp (6 g) kosher salt, divided

2 tsp (3 g) ground pepper, divided

½ cup (70 g) all-purpose flour

2 large eggs

3 tbsp (45 ml) whole milk

1 cup (50 g) panko

½ cup (57 g) finely grated Parmesan

3 tbsp (42 g) clarified butter (page 183)

½ cup (120 ml) marinara sauce, divided

1¼ cups (144 g) shredded mozzarella, divided

Chopped fresh basil, for garnish

FOR THE CREPES

In a medium mixing bowl, sift together the flour and kosher salt. In another large mixing bowl, whisk together the whole milk and the eggs. Next, add the dry ingredients one-third at a time to the wet ingredients and whisking until smooth. Then, add the butter and whisk to combine.

Place a fine mesh strainer over a large bowl. Pour the crêpe batter through the strainer and use a spatula to help move the batter through the strainer to ensure you get rid of all the lumps. Once the batter is strained, fold in the Parmesan cheese and the Italian seasoning. Cover the bowl of crêpe batter with plastic wrap and place it in the fridge for at least an hour, to overnight, for better results.

Once the crêpe batter is ready, add the vegetable oil to a 9½-inch (24-cm) crêpe pan or nonstick skillet. Using a kitchen cloth, spread the oil to coat the skillet. Then heat the skillet to medium. Take a ¼ cup (60 g) of the crêpe batter and place it into the skillet, swirling the pan to make sure the batter has spread into a large, thin pancake. Cook the crêpe on the first side until the edges start to brown which will take only about 30 seconds. Gently slide a spatula under one side of the crêpe, flip it over and continue to cook it for additional 30 seconds. Remove the crepe from the skillet and set it on a wire rack. Repeat the process until all the crêpe batter has been used.

FOR THE CHICKEN PARMESAN

While the crêpe batter rests, you can make the chicken Parmesan. Place the chicken breasts on a cutting board and cover them with plastic wrap. Using a mallet or rolling pin, flatten the chicken breasts to about ¼-inch (0.6-cm) thick. Remove the plastic wrap and then season each chicken breast with ½ teaspoon of ground oregano, ¼ teaspoon of kosher salt and ¼ teaspoon of ground pepper. Set the chicken aside.

Next, you are going to set up your breading station. In a mixing bowl or pie plate, add the flour. In another bowl, add the eggs and the milk, whisking to combine them. In another large bowl, add the panko and Parmesan cheese and stir to combine. Phew! Almost there!

Preheat a large skillet to medium-high heat and add the clarified butter. Next, take a piece of chicken and dredge it through the flour followed by the egg, shaking off any excess batter. Then dip the chicken into the panko and place it into the skillet. Repeat the process for the remaining 3 pieces of chicken. Sauté the chicken for about 7 minutes on the first side, flip and continue to cook for an additional 5 minutes or until it is thoroughly cooked. Once the chicken is cooked, remove the chicken from the skillet and place it on a wire rack.

TO ASSEMBLE

Preheat the broiler or oven to 450°F (232°C). Spray a 13 x 9-inch (33 x 23-cm) casserole dish with non-stick cooking spray. Set it aside.

Take a crêpe and lay it flat on the countertop or work surface. Place 1 chicken parmesan piece on one side of the crêpe, as if you were making a quesadilla. Top the chicken with 2 tablespoons (4 ml) of the marinara sauce and 1 tablespoon (7 g) of the mozzarella. Fold the other half of the crêpe over the chicken. Add the chicken to the prepared casserole dish. Repeat the process with the remaining 3 pieces of chicken. Once all the chicken is in the casserole top the chicken with 1 cup (113 g) of mozzarella cheese. Place the casserole into the oven and heat until the cheese is bubbly and golden brown. Remove the casserole from the oven and garnish with fresh basil.

*See photo on page 100.

Variation: Don't have time to make homemade crêpes? Grab a package of store-bought or ask your local baker for a stack.

EASY KALE QUESO

Me queso es su queso. Isn't queso a beautiful thing? Whenever we're out for Mexican food I always order chips, salsa and guacamole. Why do I hold back on the queso, you ask? Because I have zero self-control when it comes to a giant bowl of gooey cheese in front of my face. This got me thinking . . . we should all be able to have queso whenever we darn well please. Right? So, here's my answer to the queso conflict, and it's a perfectly healthy way to satisfy a craving for melted cheese. Sautéed kale mixed with garlic powder and cumin make for superior flavor, and these three ingredients serve as checkpoints to make sure you don't overdo it on the queso. Can you say winning? Or should I say dipping?

YIELDS 3 CUPS (710 ML)

NAAN BAKED CHIPS

3 whole wheat naan slices, cut into triangles (approximately 24)

2 tbsp (30 ml) olive oil

1 tsp kosher salt

1 tsp ground pepper

QUESO

1 tbsp (15 ml) olive oil

⅓ cup (70 g) minced shallot

1½ cups (51 g) finely chopped kale

¾ tsp kosher salt, divided

¾ tsp ground pepper, divided

2 tbsp (28 g) unsalted butter

2 tbsp (20 g) all-purpose flour

2 cups (264 ml) whole milk

4 oz (113 g) shredded plain havarti cheese

4 oz (113 g) shredded chipotle havarti cheese

6 oz (168 g) shredded Monterey jack cheese

¼ tsp garlic powder

¼ tsp cumin

FOR THE NAAN BAKED CHIPS

Preheat the oven to 400°F (204°C). Spray two baking sheets with non-stick cooking spray. Divide the naan chips evenly between the two baking sheets. Drizzle the olive oil, kosher salt and pepper on both sides of the chips. Place in the oven and bake for about 10 minutes or until golden brown. Remove from the oven and let them cool.

FOR THE QUESO

In a large saucepan preheated to medium-high heat, add the olive oil. Next, add the shallot and sauté for about a minute. Add the kale, ½ teaspoon of kosher salt and ½ teaspoon of pepper. Sauté the kale until softened, or for about 3 minutes. Remove the seasoned kale, and place it on a plate. In the same saucepan, melt the butter. Add the flour and whisk until a roux forms. Gradually add the milk and continue to whisk until the sauce starts to thicken, about 5 minutes. Remove the saucepan from the heat and stir in the plain havarti cheese, the chipotle havarti cheese, the Monterey jack cheese, garlic powder, cumin, ¼ teaspoon of kosher salt, ¼ teaspoon of ground pepper, the kale and shallot. Once everything is combined, pour it into a serving bowl and serve alongside naan baked chips!

Variation: Out of kale? Fresh spinach, small broccoli florets or roughly chopped collard greens make a great alternative!

BRUSCHETTA SALMON FISH STICKS

Nothing says "1980s" like fish sticks for dinner. As a girl, every Monday night I could count on squares of frozen fish hitting a baking sheet and sliding into the oven to turn crispy and golden. Topped with a little tartar sauce and a side of boxed mac and cheese, this was surely one of the decade's greatest culinary pleasures. (Okay, so maybe it wasn't as tasty as marshmallow frosting, but it's up there.) Fast forward and I still let fish sticks back into my life from time to time—albeit in a much tastier form. This recipe gets you perfectly coated salmon sticks, gently baked and then topped with a lovely bruschetta topping and balsamic drizzle. Mondays will never be the same!

SERVES 4

2 cups (298 g) halved cherry tomatoes

1 tbsp (5 g) diced shallot

1 clove garlic, minced

1 tsp balsamic vinegar

¼ cup (6 g) chopped basil

1 tsp kosher salt, divided

1 tsp ground pepper, divided

2 tbsp (20 ml) olive oil

20 oz (600 g) center-cut salmon fillet, skin removed

1 cup (125 g) all-purpose flour

1 tbsp (3 g) ground oregano

1 cup (50 g) panko

¼ cup (25 g) shredded Parmesan

2 large eggs

Balsamic glaze, for garnish

In a large bowl, add the cherry tomatoes, shallot, garlic, balsamic vinegar, basil, ½ teaspoon of kosher salt, ½ teaspoon of ground pepper and the olive oil. Toss everything together making sure all the ingredients are well combined. Place the bowl in the fridge while you make the fish sticks.

Preheat the oven to 450°F (232°C). Spray a baking sheet lined with a wire rack with non-stick cooking spray. Set it aside.

Take the salmon and cut it in half, making 2 fillets about 4 x 4 inches (10 x 10 cm) in size. Using a sharp knife, slice the fillets into 1-inch (2.5-cm) pieces and then lay the widest piece cut side down and slice in half lengthwise so you end up with a ½ x ½ x 4-inch (1 x 1 x 10-cm) fish stick.

On your countertop, set out three shallow mixing bowls or pie plates. In the first bowl, add the flour, ½ teaspoon of kosher salt, ½ teaspoon of ground pepper and the oregano, mixing well. In the second bowl, add the panko and shredded Parmesan. In the third bowl, add the eggs and whisk them. Take a piece of salmon and dip it into the flour, shaking off any excess, and then into the egg, followed by the panko. Place the salmon on the baking sheet lined with a wire rack. Repeat the dredging process until all the salmon fish sticks have been assembled. Bake the salmon fish sticks for about 7 to 10 minutes or until golden brown. Remove the fish sticks from the oven and top with a heaping spoonful of the bruschetta and a drizzle of balsamic glaze.

Kitchen Tip: Keep your bruschetta mixture in the fridge for at least 30 minutes to an hour. The longer it sits, the more flavor the tomatoes will absorb.

LOADED ZUCCHINI MEATBALL SUBS

The meatball sub: a drool-inducing, over-the-top sub that fits somewhere between "American food" and "Italian food." Probably my all-time favorite—and I'd devour one every day if I didn't have to worry about my waistline. These healthy Loaded Zucchini Meatball Subs are my way of scratching the meatball sub itch, without feeling like a human meatball for two days after. They come together really quick and are best served fully loaded, just like the original. The best part? I give you full permission to eat two or three. Your waistline will thank me!

SERVES 4

2 lb (900 g) zucchini, stems removed

1½ tsp (9 g) kosher salt, divided

1 tsp garlic powder

1 tsp onion powder

1 large whisked egg

1 cup (50 g) panko

¼ cup (45 g) grated Parmesan

1 tbsp (18 g) Italian seasoning

1 tsp ground pepper

2 tbsp (30 ml) olive oil

4 sourdough sub rolls, toasted

1 cup (240 ml) marinara sauce

1 cup (100 g) shredded mozzarella

Fresh chopped basil, for garnish

Giardiniera peppers, for garnish

Fresh grated Parmesan, for garnish

Using a medium-sized grater, grate the zucchini. Take a clean kitchen towel and place the grated zucchini on top. Sprinkle the zucchini with ½ teaspoon of kosher salt. Grab the sides of the towel and pull up. Now, either over a large bowl or over the kitchen sink, squeeze the grated zucchini to get rid of the excess water. You might have to ring the towel a couple of times to make sure all the moisture is gone.

Once you've squeezed the excess water out, place the dry zucchini into a clean mixing bowl. Add in the garlic powder, onion powder, egg, panko, Parmesan, Italian seasoning, 1 teaspoon of kosher salt and 1 teaspoon of ground pepper. Using a fork, toss gently until the mixture is thoroughly combined. Then, take a small ice cream scoop, or your hands, and form the zucchini mixture into 1-inch (2.5-cm) balls. Place the "meatballs" on a plate and set it aside.

In a large skillet preheated to medium heat, add the olive oil. Using a pair of tongs, add the zucchini meatballs to the skillet and fry them on all sides for about 7 to 10 minutes. Remove the meatballs from the skillet and place them on a plate lined with a paper towel.

To assemble the subs, take a toasted sub roll and place 3 zucchini meatballs into the middle. Pour some of the marinara sauce over the zucchini and top it with ¼ cup (25 g) of the mozzarella cheese. Place the sub on a baking sheet. Repeat the process until all the subs have been assembled.

Turn your broiler on. Place the baking sheet under the broiler until the cheese has turned slightly golden brown and the subs are toasted. Remove the baking sheet from the broiler and garnish the subs with fresh basil, Giardiniera peppers and Parmesan.

Variation: If you want to keep this meal low-carb, simply omit the sub rolls and serve the meatballs over your favorite marinara sauce.

BEEF WELLINGTON-STUFFED ACORN SQUASH

When I think beef wellington, I think tradition. I imagine it served at an elegant restaurant with white linens and sparkling glassware. Servers in tuxes waltz around the tables as if they're in a synchronized dance, and martinis are being shaken, not stirred. I love the grand ceremony of fine dining, but maybe it's time beef wellington had a wardrobe change. This version will razzle and dazzle you and the in-laws, too. All the usual suspects make an appearance—beef tenderloin, Dijon mustard, ham, mushrooms, rosemary and puff pastry. But this version takes all the delicious ingredients and stuffs them into roasted acorn squashes. Serve it all up at your next dinner party and your guests will be waltzing their applause.

SERVES 4

4 medium-sized acorn squash

5 tbsp (75 ml) olive oil, divided

¾ tsp kosher salt, divided

¾ tsp ground pepper, divided

2 tbsp (28 g) clarified butter (page 183)

1 lb (450 g) beef tenderloin steaks

1 tbsp (18 g) Dijon mustard

1 cup (150 g) diced yellow onion

1 cup (110 g) chopped baby bella mushrooms

2 tsp (2 g) chopped fresh rosemary

1 tbsp (4 g) chopped fresh thyme

1 tbsp (15 ml) white wine

1½ cups (293 g) cooked brown rice

3 tbsp (45 ml) heavy cream

1 sheet puff pastry rolled and cut into 4½-inch (11-cm) squares

1 large egg, whisked

Fresh chives, for garnish

Preheat the oven to 400°F (204°C).

Take an acorn squash and slice a thin piece off the bottom so the squash will stand up straight when baked. Then slice off the tops of the acorn squash, about a quarter of the way down. You want to be able to create a well to be able to stuff later. Remove the seeds. Drizzle the tops and inside of each squash with 1 tablespoon (15 ml) of olive oil, ¼ teaspoon of kosher salt and ¼ teaspoon of ground pepper. Roast the squash on a baking sheet for about 30 minutes or until it is tender. Remove the squash from the oven and set it aside.

Meanwhile, preheat a skillet to medium-high heat and add the clarified butter. Sprinkle the steak with ¼ teaspoon of kosher salt and ¼ teaspoon of ground pepper. Add the steak to the skillet and cook for about 3 minutes per side. Remove the steak from the skillet and brush each side with 1 tablespoon (18 g) of Dijon mustard. Let the steak rest before cutting it into cubes.

In the same skillet you cooked the steak in, add the mushrooms. Sauté the mushrooms until golden brown, or about 3 minutes. Add the onion, 1 tablespoon (15 ml) of olive oil, the rosemary, thyme, ¼ teaspoon of kosher salt and ¼ teaspoon of ground pepper. Sauté the veggies until they soften. Deglaze the skillet with the white wine and then add the cooked rice, chopped steak and cream. Stir to combine and heat through.

Divide the beef wellington mixture among the 4 acorn squash. Take a piece of puff pastry and place it on top of each of the acorn squash. Brush the tops with the egg wash. Using a fork, prick a few holes in the top of the puff pastry to keep it from rising. Place the squash back in the oven for about 10 minutes or until the puff pastry is golden. Remove the squash from the oven and garnish the tops with chives.

Kitchen Tip: Use up the leftover stuffing by adding it to zucchini boats for a tasty next day lunch!

RED BEANS AND RICE BURGER

If I could swim in a giant bowl of traditional Louisiana red beans and rice—yep, I would. Don't judge, y'all! This flavorful, hearty dish is one of my favorites when I'm below the Mason-Dixon line. Slow-cooked beans and rice, mixed with andouille sausage, go beyond your belly, right to the soul. And though I'd happily go on a red beans and rice bender, this vegetarian burger is a deliciously easy compromise. It's got all the flavors of the authentic dish, with half the effort—perfect for weekdays, yet sassy enough for impromptu dinner parties!

SERVES 6

⅓ cup (77 g) mayonnaise

1 tbsp (6 g) Creole mustard

1 tbsp (6 g) sliced scallions

1 tbsp (15 ml) lemon juice

2 (15-oz [840-g]) cans dark red kidney beans, drained and rinsed

1¼ cups (200 g) cooked white rice

½ cup (90 g) diced red pepper

⅓ cup (35 g) diced celery

⅓ cup (35 g) diced shallot

1 cup (50 g) panko

1½ tbsp (9 g) Cajun seasoning

1 tsp garlic powder

½ tsp red pepper flakes

1½ tsp (16 g) kosher salt, divided

1½ tsp (16 g) ground pepper, divided

3 large eggs, whisked

2 tbsp (30 ml) olive oil

6 slices medium sharp white cheddar cheese

6 pieces butter lettuce

6 tomato slices

6 brioche buns, toasted

To make the Creole aioli, in a medium bowl, combine the mayonnaise, Creole mustard, scallions, lemon juice, ¼ teaspoon of kosher salt and ¼ teaspoon of ground pepper. Place the bowl in the fridge for at least 20 minutes to allow the flavors to combine.

In a large bowl, add the kidney beans and, using a potato masher, mash them. Next, add the cooked rice, red pepper, celery, shallot, panko, Cajun seasoning, garlic powder, red pepper flakes, 1 teaspoon of kosher salt and 1 teaspoon of ground pepper along with the eggs.

Mix until well combined. If the bean mixture seems too wet, add more panko. This will help with binding and keep the burger from falling apart when cooking. Take the red bean mixture and form it into five to six ½-inch (1-cm) patties.

Preheat a large cast-iron skillet to medium-high heat. Add the olive oil and cook the burger patties about 5 minutes on each side until they are golden brown. In the last minute of cooking, add a slice of cheese on top of each burger patty and let the cheese melt. Once the cheese has melted, place the patties on a plate. Repeat the process with the remaining burger patties.

To assemble the burgers, place the red beans and rice burger on top of a brioche bun. Top the burger with a piece of butter lettuce, a tomato slice and 1 tablespoon (15 ml) of the Creole aioli. Cap the burger with the remaining top bun. Repeat the process until all the burgers have been assembled.

Kitchen Tip: Place the burgers in the fridge for an hour before cooking to firm them up. This will keep the burgers from falling apart and will allow the flavors to come through.

SPANISH WEDGE SALAD

Ah, the wedge. This classic "comfort salad" has been around since the 1950s. It was the star of the salad world before folks knew about the likes of romaine, endive or arugula. The wedge was ultimately shunned from the foodie kingdom because, well, it's iceberg. Deemed the least nutritious, sad-looking lettuce on the grocery store shelf, people fled from iceberg lettuce to greener pastures. I'm happily bringing this nostalgic salad back to the forefront with a Spanish twist. The wedges are still the foundation, I'm just upping the ingredients— instead of bacon, I add chorizo, and instead of blue cheese, I add shredded Manchego. It's all topped off with a big drizzle of sassy green-olive vinaigrette. Iceberg is back!

SERVES 4

½ lb (230 g) freshly ground pork chorizo

¼ cup (60 ml) olive oil

¼ cup (60 ml) red wine vinegar

¼ cup (32 g) chopped Spanish green olives

¼ cup (6 g) chopped fresh basil

⅓ cup (50 g) chopped red onion

½ tsp kosher salt

½ tsp ground pepper

1 head iceberg lettuce, cut into 4 wedges

4 hard-boiled eggs, peeled and sliced

1 cup (152 g) chickpeas, rinsed and drained

½ cup (57 g) shredded Manchego cheese

¼ cup (35 g) roughly chopped Marcona almonds

Fresh chopped parsley, for garnish

In a medium skillet preheated to medium-high heat, add the chorizo. Using a wooden spoon, break up the chorizo and continue to cook until the meat is no longer pink, or about 5 minutes. Remove the chorizo from the skillet with a slotted spoon and set it aside in a bowl to cool.

Meanwhile, make the olive vinaigrette. Add the olive oil, red wine vinegar, green olives, basil, red onion, kosher salt and ground pepper to a large bowl. Whisk all the ingredients together and set them aside.

To assemble the wedge salad, place a wedge of iceberg lettuce on a plate. Top the wedge with some of the chorizo, 1 sliced hard-boiled egg, ¼ cup (38 g) of the chickpeas, ¼ cup (29 g) of the Manchego cheese, 1 tablespoon (9 g) of the Marcona almonds and a drizzle of the olive vinaigrette. Repeat this process until all the wedges have been assembled. Dive in!

Kitchen Tip: The vinaigrette will taste better as the day goes on and will keep for up to a week in the fridge.

Variation: Romaine lettuce would be a lovely substitute for iceberg!

CHICKEN AND ANDOUILLE
with CARROT NOODLES

I'd never experienced true Southern food until I met Mr. B. While half his ancestry hails from Dixie, I fit the Yankee stereotype to a T, completely ignorant of blissful dishes like shrimp and grits, po' boys or shrimp Creole. When at last I got a taste of Southern hospitality, I fell in love with the flavors and spices. Garlic, paprika, cayenne, oregano, thyme and red pepper flakes—my palate hadn't a clue what to do. Except to ask for seconds! I may be considered a Yank, but I still love going Southern in the kitchen. Chicken and Andouille with Carrot Noodles is a simple roux mixed with andouille, a vegetable trinity and strings of carrot. It's a perfect entry-level course that even tried and true Southerners will love.

SERVES 4

4 tbsp (56 g) unsalted butter, divided

½ lb (260 g) skinless, boneless chicken breast, cut into 1-inch (2.5-cm) cubes

1½ tsp (9 g) kosher salt, divided

1½ tsp (5 g) ground pepper, divided

1 cup (104 g) chopped red onion

½ cup (90 g) chopped green pepper

½ cup (90 g) chopped red pepper

2 celery ribs, chopped

2 cloves garlic, minced

¼ cup (36 g) all-purpose flour

2 andouille sausage links, pre-cooked (about 6 oz [260 g]), sliced on the bias into ½-inch (1.3-cm) pieces

1 tbsp (16 g) tomato paste

1½ tbsp (12 g) Cajun seasoning

¼ tsp red pepper flakes

2¼ cups (500 ml) chicken stock

4 cups (440 g) carrot noodles (page 183)

Fresh chopped parsley, for garnish

In a large cast-iron skillet preheated to medium-high heat, melt 1 tablespoon (14 g) of the butter. Add the chicken cubes, ½ teaspoon of kosher salt and ½ teaspoon of ground pepper. Stir to combine. Sauté the chicken for about 4 to 5 minutes or until it is no longer pink inside. Remove the chicken from the skillet with a slotted spoon. Place the chicken on a plate and set it aside.

In the same cast-iron skillet, melt the remaining 3 tablespoons (42 g) of the butter. Next, add the onion, green pepper, red pepper, celery and garlic. Stir to combine, and add 1 teaspoon of kosher salt and 1 teaspoon of ground pepper. Continue to stir the veggies until they are softened, or for about 5 minutes. Add the flour and continue to stir as you cook out the flour. Next, add the andouille sausage, tomato paste, Cajun seasoning and red pepper flakes. The andouille mixture will be thick and that's okay! Continue to cook for about 2 minutes making sure everything is well combined. Next, add the chicken broth and cooked chicken into the skillet and simmer until the sauce starts to thicken, which takes about 5 minutes.

Meanwhile, bring a pot filled with salted water to boil. Add the carrot noodles to the pot and cook them for about 3 to 5 minutes. Once cooked, drain the noodles into a colander. Divide the carrot noodles among four bowls and ladle the chicken and andouille sauce over the carrot noodles. Garnish with parsley.

Variation: You can prepare the carrot noodles ahead of time by draining the cooked noodles and then shocking them in cold water. This will stop the cooking process and help retain the bright orange color. Simply reheat before serving.

SPICED HONEY-BARBECUE BAKED CORNISH HENS

I make barbecue chicken for dinner at least once a week. It's that easy, don't-have-to-think-about-it dish you can switch up using a thigh, drumstick (fav!), chicken breast or wing, and no one would know the difference. But I hadn't considered using cornish hens until last Christmas when my brother-in-law made a smorgasbord of meats—one of which was that cute little bird you find wrapped in plastic at the grocery store. He smoked the cornish hens on a grill and I must say, they were juicy, slightly crisp on the outside and bursting with flavor. Who knew a bird could taste so good? This Spiced Honey-Barbecue Baked Cornish Hen is my attempt to make cornish hen a weeknight staple in your house. Simply brush the honey barbecue sauce on the cornish hen, roast for 30 minutes and voilà! A giant chicken wing—er, I mean, a delicious bird—that is finger-licking good and ready in less than an hour!

SERVES 4

4 cornish hens, about 1 lb (453 g) each, legs tied together with kitchen twine

¼ cup (60 ml) olive oil, divided

1 tbsp (17 g) kosher salt, divided

1 tbsp (6 g) ground pepper, divided

2 cups (480 ml) barbecue sauce

1 cup (240 ml) honey

¼ cup (60 ml) ketchup

¼ cup (60 ml) hot sauce

8 tbsp (112 g) unsalted butter

1 tsp garlic powder

1 tsp ground paprika

¼ tsp cayenne

Fresh parsley, for garnish

Preheat the oven to 350°F (177°C).

In a 12-inch (30-cm) cast-iron skillet, add the cornish hens. Season each of the cornish hens with 1 tablespoon (15 ml) of the olive oil, 1 teaspoon of kosher salt and 1 teaspoon of ground pepper. Place the skillet into the oven and roast it for 40 minutes.

While the hens roast, make the honey barbecue sauce. In a saucepan preheated to medium heat, add the barbecue sauce, honey, ketchup, hot sauce, butter, garlic powder and paprika. Stir all the ingredients together until well combined. Simmer the sauce for about 5 to 7 minutes or until the sauce has reduced a little.

Using an oven mitt, remove the skillet of cornish hens from the oven. Using a pastry brush, brush the sauce all over the cornish hens. Place the skillet back in the oven and continue to roast for another 20 minutes or until the inner thigh of the hen registers 160°F (71°C).

Transfer the hens to a cutting board and let them rest for about 5 to 10 minutes. You can either serve the hens whole or slice the meat off and serve. Garnish with the parsley.

Kitchen Tip: Let the cornish hens sit outside the fridge at room temperature for at least an hour before roasting. This will help to ensure the hens cook evenly.

Variation: If you want to make the honey barbecue sauce less spicy, dial back the hot sauce to about 2 tablespoons (30 ml).

CAULIFLOWER CLAM CHOWDER
with CRISPY BACON

How do you like your "chowdah"? I'll take mine with a giant pale ale and a smile, please. Carrots, celery, onion and potatoes thickened with butter, flour, milk and chicken stock: it's pure comfort in a bowl. But! If you're like me and you love to tinker, try using cauliflower instead of potatoes. Cauliflower florets still hold a hearty tune when used as a base for many dishes, soups included. Add in some trusty clams and you've got a satisfying meal in about 30 minutes!

SERVES 4

3 slices bacon

3 tbsp (42 g) unsalted butter

½ cup (50 g) chopped celery

½ cup (64 g) peeled and chopped carrots

1 cup (150 g) chopped yellow onion

1 lb (450 g) cauliflower head, chopped into florets

1½ tsp (16 g) garlic powder

¼ tsp red pepper flakes

1 tsp kosher salt

1 tsp ground pepper

3 tbsp (24 g) all-purpose flour

1¼ cups (300 ml) whole milk

3 cups (720 ml) chicken stock

½ cup (120 ml) clam juice

1 bay leaf

¾ cup (169 g) canned baby clams, drained

Chopped fresh parsley, for garnish

In a large Dutch oven preheated to medium-high heat, add the bacon slices. Sauté the bacon for about 5 to 6 minutes or until it becomes crispy. Remove the bacon from the Dutch oven with tongs and set it on a plate lined with a paper towel to cool. Once cool, chop the bacon and set it aside.

Remove 2 tablespoons (30 ml) of excess bacon fat from the Dutch oven. Keeping the temperature at medium-high heat, melt the butter. Next, add the celery, carrots and onion. Sauté the veggies for a few minutes or until they become slightly softened. Next, add the cauliflower, garlic powder, red pepper flakes, kosher salt and ground pepper. Using a wooden spoon, stir all the veggies and spices together making sure everything is well combined. Cook for another couple of minutes. Then add the flour and continue to stir until the flour has cooked out—about a minute. Gradually pour in the milk, chicken stock, clam juice and add the bay leaf. Stir the mixture until it is well combined and bring it to a boil. Once at a boil, turn the chowder to a simmer. Simmer the chowder for about 15 minutes, or until it begins to thicken. Remove the bay leaf and add the chopped bacon back into the chowder along with the clams. Give one final, big stir and taste to make sure seasoning is to your liking. Add more salt and pepper, if desired. To serve, ladle the chowder into bowls and garnish with the parsley.

Kitchen Tip: This chowder is a great meal to make ahead and freeze when you need dinner in a hurry!

BISON SKILLET MEATBALLS *with* HATCH CHILE VERDE

I feel spoiled living in Colorado. Majestic mountains to the west, favorable weather most of the year (no humidity!), and access to an endless supply of Hatch chiles. When I first moved to Denver, the late-summer Hatch chile stands on every corner were an oddity. However, all it took was one bite of these buttery, slightly smoky Hatch chiles and I was hooked. To pay homage to the Hatch chile and all its delicious glory, I decided to introduce it to one of my favorite comfort foods: the meatball. We have bison in Colorado too, so naturally I thought a bison meatball would complement the Hatch chile. All you have to do is set up the standard meatball mixing station and place them in a hot tub full of Hatch chile verde. Now you can get your Hatch chile fix all year long!

SERVES 4

2 cups (480 ml) chicken stock

1 lb (450 g) tomatillos, husked, rinsed, cut into ½-inch (1.3-cm) wedges

1 lb (450 g) mild Hatch chiles, peeled, seeded, diced and roasted

6 cloves garlic, peeled

1 cup (150 g) diced yellow onion

1 cup (16 g) fresh packed cilantro

2 tsp (4 g) ground cumin, divided

2 tsp (4 g) Mexican oregano, divided

1 tsp ground coriander

2¼ tsp (17 g) kosher salt, divided

2 tsp (9 g) ground pepper, divided

2 lb (908 g) ground bison

1 cup (50 g) panko

½ cup (75 g) grated yellow onion

2 large eggs, whisked

¼ cup (28 g) grated Manchego cheese

1 tsp garlic powder

1 tbsp (14 g) clarified butter (page 183)

To make the Hatch chile verde sauce, in a large food processor or blender, add the chicken stock, tomatillos, Hatch chiles, garlic, diced onion, cilantro, 1 teaspoon of cumin, 1 teaspoon of Mexican oregano, coriander, 1 teaspoon of kosher salt and 1 teaspoon of ground pepper. Pulse until combined and smooth. Set the sauce aside.

To make the meatballs, in a large mixing bowl, add the bison, panko, grated onion, eggs, Manchego, 1 teaspoon of cumin, 1 teaspoon of Mexican oregano, garlic powder, 1¼ teaspoons (8 g) of kosher salt and 1 teaspoon of ground pepper. Start mixing the bison mixture with your hands. Keep mixing until all the ingredients are well incorporated. The mixture may be a little wet, but that's okay!

Using an ice cream scoop, or about 1½ tablespoons (21 g) of the meat mixture, portion the meat into a meatball and place the meatballs onto a baking sheet. Once all the meatballs are formed, place the baking sheet into the fridge and allow the meatballs to set for about 30 minutes to an hour.

Once the meatballs are about set, preheat a large skillet with a lid to medium heat. Add the hatch chile verde sauce to the skillet and simmer for a few minutes allowing some of the liquid to sweat out. Keep the sauce warm until ready to garnish it with the meatballs.

Preheat a separate large skillet to medium-high heat. Add the clarified butter to the skillet. Next, add the meatballs, a few at a time, and sear them on both sides until they are golden brown, or about 2 to 3 minutes. Once the meatballs are seared, place them into the skillet with the Hatch chile verde sauce.

Cover the skillet with a lid and cook the meatballs for about 15 minutes over medium-high heat until they are warmed through.

Variation: If you can't find fresh Hatch chiles you can substitute with two 4-oz (113-g) cans of diced green chiles. Also, ground beef is an excellent substitute if you can't find bison.

SWEET POTATO NOODLE CHICKEN PUTTANESCA

Back in the day, I remember dining at a certain Italian restaurant where all-you-could-eat breadsticks and salad were on the house. You'd think that mercilessly stuffing oneself with bowls of iceberg lettuce and buttery carb sticks would leave little room for an entrée, but I still managed to squeeze in a couple of bites of chicken Parmesan. How? By eliminating dignity, my friends. I remember leaving the restaurant thinking . . . never again. This Chicken Puttanesca Sweet Potato Noodle Skillet is the answer to that "I'll just have a bite of endless salad and breadsticks" losing scenario. Sautéed chicken is mixed with tomatoes, olives and capers, then smothered over sweet potato noodles. This skillet is light and flavorful, leaving you with just the right amount of room to warrant another breadstick.

SERVES 4

2 tbsp (29 g) clarified butter (page 183)

4 (8-oz [220-g]) skinless, boneless chicken breasts

1¼ tsp (8 g) kosher salt, divided

1¼ tsp (4 g) ground pepper, divided

¼ cup (60 ml) dry white wine

1½ cups (188 g) diced yellow onion

2 cloves garlic, minced

1 cup (149 g) grape tomatoes, halved

2 tbsp (33 g) tomato paste

½ tsp red pepper flakes

½ tsp Italian seasoning

½ cup (119 ml) chicken broth

1 cup (180 g) black olives, pitted, sliced in half

1 tbsp (9 g) capers, drained

¼ cup (6 g) fresh basil, chopped, plus more for garnish

1 tbsp (15 ml) olive oil

1 tbsp (14 g) unsalted butter

4 cups (532 g) sweet potato noodles (page 183)

To prepare the chicken breasts, preheat a large Dutch oven to medium-high heat and add the clarified butter. Sprinkle each chicken breast with ¼ teaspoon of kosher salt and ¼ teaspoon of ground pepper, making sure each side is well-seasoned. Add the chicken to the pan and sear it on both sides until it is slightly golden, or for about 4 to 5 minutes. Remove the chicken from the Dutch oven and place it on a plate.

To make the puttanesca sauce, add the white wine to the Dutch oven to deglaze the pan, which releases all the browned bits from the chicken that are stuck to the bottom of the pot to flavor the sauce. Next, add the onions and sauté for 5 minutes, or until they are softened. Add the garlic and cook for additional 30 seconds. Once you can smell the garlic, add the tomatoes, tomato paste, red pepper flakes, Italian seasoning, ¼ teaspoon of kosher salt and ¼ teaspoon of ground pepper. Stir the mixture to combine it and then pour in the chicken broth. Cover the tomato mixture and simmer it for about 7 minutes or until it is slightly thickened.

Finally, stir in the black olives, capers and more chicken broth if the mixture is too thick. Add the chicken breast back to the pan, cover and cook for another 10 to 12 minutes, or until the chicken is no longer pink inside. Once cooked, stir in the fresh basil and remove the Dutch oven from the heat.

Meanwhile, preheat a large skillet to medium-high. Add the olive oil and the butter to the pan. Once the butter is melted, add the sweet potato noodles. Sauté until the noodles are tender, about 5 minutes. Season the noodles with salt and pepper, if desired. Remove the noodles from the pan and divide the sweet potato noodles among four bowls. Place a chicken breast on top of each bowl of noodles, followed by the puttanesca sauce. Serve with more fresh basil.

Variation: To add a little extra zing to this dish, try using marinated spicy olives from the olive bar at the grocery store.

Modern Drive-Thru

"May I take your order?"

It's a question I remember hearing only a handful of times during childhood. Growing up in the '80s, fast food was very different. Or at least it felt different. I remember my mother treating my brothers and me to juicy cheeseburgers and golden French fries for dinner only when my father was out of town on business. Eating out was reserved for special occasions, and was something to be savored.

Fast forward to my college years and that question of ordering out became quite the norm. Breakfast sandwiches on-the-go, waiting in line for a giant meat-filled burrito or craving a box of French fries with a chocolate shake for extra dipping pleasure was standard behavior. Thankfully I grew out of my three-meals-a-day fast food fixation and went back to treating it like a special occasion.

I adore fast food, but we now have so many other accessible ingredients that things should change. This chapter is my version of what a Modern Drive-Thru should look and taste like. From Chorizo Cheeseburgers (page 145) to Fried Squash Rings (page 153) to Bacon and Blue Cheese Brussels Sprout Tater Tots (page 142), this drive-thru menu is bursting with flavor and worthy of a friendly, "May I take your order?"

BACON BLUE CHEESE BRUSSELS SPROUT TATER TOTS

I've never met a tater tot I didn't like. There's something about those golden, baked or fried potato gems that brings out the five-year-old kid in me. We had tots on the table growing up, served alongside tuna casserole, sloppy joes or chicken nuggets. But as an adult my palate has expanded, and I figure it's time to give tater tots a proper makeover. This version mixes tots, crispy bacon, blue cheese and brussels sprouts, and covers it all in a decadent maple butter. Your five-year-old self will be giddy with delight, and the fancy-pants adult in you will be pretty pleased, too.

YIELDS 20 TATER TOTS

2 slices bacon

2 cups (88 g) finely shredded Brussels sprouts

⅔ cup (80 g) panko

1 shallot, diced

⅓ cup (45 g) blue cheese crumbles

2 eggs, whisked

1 tbsp (9 g) all-purpose flour

¼ tsp salt

¼ tsp pepper

1 tbsp (14 g) unsalted butter

1 tbsp (15 ml) maple syrup

Preheat the oven to 425°F (218°C)

Preheat a skillet to medium-high heat. Add the bacon slices to the skillet and cook until they are crispy. Remove the bacon from the skillet with a pair of tongs, leaving the bacon fat. Place the bacon on a plate lined with a paper towel until it is cool enough to dice. In the same skillet, add the Brussels sprouts. Cook the Brussels sprouts in the bacon fat for about 1 to 2 minutes. Turn off the skillet and place the Brussels sprouts into a large mixing bowl. Let the Brussels sprouts cool slightly before adding in the remaining ingredients.

Once the sprouts have cooled, add the bacon, panko, shallot, blue cheese, eggs, flour, salt and pepper to the Brussels sprouts. Mix until everything is well combined. Line a baking sheet with a silicone baking mat. Using an ice cream scoop, scoop about 1½ tablespoons (8 g) of the brussels sprout mixture and form it into a tater tot. You may need to wash your hands in between forming the tots to make it easier. Keep pressing and shaping the mixture until the tater tot takes form. Place the tater tots on the baking sheet and bake them for about 18 minutes, or until they are golden brown, flipping them halfway through the cooking time. Meanwhile, melt the butter in a microwave. Once the butter is melted, add the maple syrup and stir to combine. Remove the tater tots from the oven, brush the tops with the maple butter and serve them immediately!

Kitchen Tip: Have leftover tater tots? Simply save them in an airtight container and place them in the fridge for up to 24 hours. To reheat, just preheat your oven to 325°F (163°C), place the tater tots on a baking sheet and heat them until warm, or about 5 minutes.

CHORIZO CHEESEBURGER *with* CHIMICHURRI AIOLI

My love for chorizo runs deep. Like, I've reached "fangirl" status. It's totally normal to have a crush on a piece of food that you consume, right? There's something so sexy and sassy about chorizo—it should really have its own food group. If you've never tried this Spanish sausage, you'll find it's full of spice, but not heat. You'll typically find chorizo ground, or in a casing link at the grocery store meat counter. Being a fangirl, I decided to give chorizo a new look, putting it right at the heart of fast-food cuisine. No more dry burgers and sad faces. Instead of large-sizing a #3 combo, how about a mixture of ground chorizo, beef and a slice of cheese topped with swoon-worthy chimichurri aioli? I'd happily pull up to the second window for that.

SERVES 4

CHORIZO CHEESEBURGER

1 lb (453 g) ground beef

1 lb (453 g) freshly ground pork chorizo

1 tsp kosher salt

1 tsp kosher pepper

1 tsp hot sauce

1 tbsp (14 g) clarified butter (page 183)

4 brioche buns

4 slices white cheddar cheese

Shredded lettuce, for garnish

Tomato slices, for garnish

CHIMICHURRI AIOLI

½ cup fresh parsley

¼ cup (60 ml) olive oil

¼ cup (60 ml) red wine vinegar

2 tbsp (8 g) chopped fresh cilantro

¼ cup (16 g) chopped fresh mint

1 clove garlic, peeled

¼ tsp red pepper flakes

¼ tsp ground cumin

¼ tsp kosher salt

¼ tsp ground pepper

1 cup (232 g) mayonnaise

FOR THE CHORIZO CHEESEBURGER

In a large bowl, combine the ground beef, ground chorizo, kosher salt, ground pepper and hot sauce. Using your hands, shape four 4-inch (10-cm) chorizo hamburger patties.

Next, preheat a cast-iron skillet to medium heat. Add the clarified butter to the skillet. Then place the four chorizo patties into the skillet. Cook the patties for about 5 to 6 minutes on the first side, flip and cook an additional 3 minutes for medium-rare burgers. If you would like the burgers more well-done, cook an additional 4 to 5 minutes. In the last minute of cooking, place the white cheddar cheese slices on top of the chorizo patties to melt. Once cooked, place the chorizo patties on a plate to rest before serving.

FOR THE CHIMICHURRI AIOLI

In a small food processer or blender, add the parsley, olive oil, red wine vinegar, cilantro, mint, garlic, red pepper flakes, cumin, salt and pepper. Pulse until smooth. In a bowl, add 2½ tablespoons (36 ml) of the chimichurri to the mayo. Combine well and set aside.

To serve, place a chorizo cheeseburger patty on the bottom of a brioche bun. Top with the chimichurri aioli, lettuce, tomato and top of the brioche bun. Repeat the process to make the remaining three burgers.

Variation: If you can't find freshly ground chorizo at the grocery store, you can certainly sub in ground turkey, pork, chicken or lamb!

BLUEBERRY CHIA PANCAKES *with* MAPLE BUTTER SYRUP

They say breakfast is the most important meal of the day. If "they" are telling the truth, you'll want to start committing daily to these Blueberry Chia Pancakes with Maple Butter Syrup. Forget dry, lukewarm flapjacks tossed inside those weird Styrofoam™ containers, and spend a little extra time whipping up these fluffy breakfast-cakes. They're made with gluten-free flour, frozen blueberries, chia seeds, cinnamon and lemon zest. Drizzle the tops with maple butter syrup, and you'll start your day off right.

SERVES 4

MAPLE BUTTER SYRUP

4 tbsp (56 g) unsalted butter

4 tbsp (60 ml) maple syrup

1 tsp lemon zest

BLUEBERRY CHIA PANCAKES

2 cups (480 g) almond flour

½ tsp kosher salt

½ tsp ground cinnamon

4 large eggs

1 tsp vanilla extract

2 tbsp (20 g) chia seeds

2 tsp (4 g) lemon zest

1 cup (237 ml) water

1 cup (150 g) fresh blueberries

FOR THE MAPLE BUTTER SYRUP

In a small saucepan, melt the butter over medium heat. Stir in the maple syrup and lemon zest. Keep stirring until the butter, maple syrup and lemon zest have been combined. Turn the heat to low and keep it warm until it is ready to serve with the pancakes.

FOR THE BLUEBERRY CHIA PANCAKES

In a bowl, mix together the flour, kosher salt and cinnamon. In another large bowl, whisk together egg, vanilla extract, chia seeds, lemon zest and water. Add the wet ingredients to the dry ingredients. Gently fold in the blueberries.

Preheat a skillet to medium heat and spray it with non-stick cooking spray. Take ¼ cup (21 g) of the pancake batter and ladle it into the skillet. Once tiny bubbles appear on top of the pancake, after about 2 to 3 minutes, flip and continue to cook until golden brown, or about a minute or two. Repeat this process until all the pancake batter has been used. Serve it with warm maple butter syrup.

Kitchen Tip: These pancakes can be made ahead and frozen. They are easy to reheat and eat during the busy work week!

BAKED LEMON CHICKEN NUGGETS
with MUSTARD TAHINI DIPPING SAUCE

When it comes to ordering fast food, you're either on team burger or team nugget. There's no real in-between, because no one orders a salad from the drive-thru, right? I've always been on team burger. But every now and then I get a hankering for chicken nuggets. I think I'm mesmerized by the ability to dunk a small piece of golden chicken into a variety of condiments. These Baked Lemon Chicken Nuggets with Mustard Tahini Dipping Sauce are far superior to the box of nuggets you'll find in the drive-thru. Baked lemon nuggets are a healthier option, and the mustard tahini dipping sauce is amazingly flavorful. Mix tahini with some mustard and lemon juice, and you'll be dipping right on over to team chicken nugget.

SERVES 4

1 cup (125 g) all-purpose flour

2 large eggs

1½ cups (75 g) panko

2 tsp (4 g) lemon zest

2 tsp (4 g) lemon pepper

½ cup (57 g) grated Parmesan

1¼ tsp (8 g) kosher salt, divided

1 tsp ground pepper

2 lb (900 g) boneless, skinless chicken breasts cut into 1-inch (2.5-cm) cubes

¼ cup (60 ml) tahini

2 tbsp (30 ml) Dijon mustard

2 tbsp (30 ml) apple cider vinegar

¼ cup (60 ml) water

1 tbsp (15 ml) lemon juice

2 tsp (10 ml) honey

Preheat the oven to 425°F (218°C). Spray a baking sheet with non-stick cooking spray and set it aside.

Next, add the flour to a mixing bowl. In another bowl, add the eggs and whisk. In a third bowl, add the panko, lemon zest, lemon pepper, Parmesan cheese, 1 teaspoon of kosher salt and the ground pepper, stirring to ensure everything is well combined.

Take a chicken nugget and dip it into the flour. Shake off any excess flour and dip it into the whisked egg, then the seasoned panko. You may need to press the panko mixture into the chicken, just to make sure it sticks. Once the chicken nugget has been coated, place it on the baking sheet. Repeat until all the chicken nuggets have been coated.

Place the baking sheet into the oven and bake the chicken nuggets for about 10 to 14 minutes, making sure to flip them halfway through.

While the chicken nuggets bake, assemble the mustard tahini dipping sauce. In a small bowl, whisk together the tahini, Dijon mustard, apple cider vinegar, water, lemon juice, honey and remaining ¼ teaspoon of kosher salt. If the sauce is too thick, add water until the desired consistency is reached.

Once baked, remove the chicken nuggets from the oven and serve them with mustard tahini dipping sauce.

Variation: Have some fun with these chicken nuggets and mix up the spices! Try adding cumin, turmeric, paprika or coriander to the panko mixture to kick things up a notch!

BERRY HEMP PORRIDGE PARFAITS

Whenever I hear the word "porridge," I think of Goldilocks and the Three Bears. As a six-year-old I thought to myself, why is Goldilocks eating porridge? She needs a bowl of Frosted Flakes, a stack of pancakes or a strawberry pop tart. No one eats porridge! Eventually, I grew out my sugar-fix breakfast phase, but these Berry Hemp Porridge Parfaits are made to satisfy both adult and kiddo tastes. The base of the porridge is made with hemp seeds, which are one of the earliest cultivated plants and a great source of protein! Making porridge is like creating oatmeal on the stovetop. Add water, milk and whatever spices you prefer like cinnamon or nutmeg. Make the porridge, layer in Greek yogurt, some berries and serve! Fill a few to-go containers for a fast and easy breakfast that Goldilocks would find "just right"!

SERVES 4

1¼ cups (305 ml) whole milk

¾ cup (93 g) raw, shelled hemp seeds

1 tbsp (11 g) chia seeds

1 tbsp (15 ml) honey, plus extra for garnish

½ tsp vanilla extract

1 tsp brown sugar

½ tsp ground cinnamon

¼ tsp kosher salt

2 cups (470 g) plain Greek yogurt

2 cups (300 g) halved fresh strawberries

2 cups (300 g) fresh blueberries

2 cups (288 g) fresh blackberries

2 cups (250 g) fresh raspberries

In a saucepan add the whole milk, hemp seeds, chia seeds, honey, vanilla exact, brown sugar, cinnamon and kosher salt. Stir everything together until it is well combined. Bring the porridge mixture to a boil over medium heat. Keep stirring the porridge and then reduce the heat to medium-low. Simmer the porridge until it is thickened, or for about 4 to 7 minutes. Remove the saucepan from the heat and let the porridge come to almost room temperature because you don't want the Greek yogurt to curdle when you are assembling it.

In the bottom of a tall glass, add ¼ cup (60 g) of Greek yogurt followed by the strawberries, blueberries, blackberries and raspberries. Top the fruit with ¼ cup (23 g) of the porridge mixture. Repeat the layering one more time. Top the final layer with a dollop of Greek yogurt and more fruit. Drizzle with honey. Repeat the process until all the glasses have been filled.

Kitchen Tip: You can use frozen fruit that has been partially thawed and then plop it into your parfait glass for a nice snap of cold!

FRIED SQUASH RINGS

When it comes to fast-food onion rings, I'm a sucker for Sonic. That, and their crushed ice. I don't know how they do those onion rings, but they're always perfectly fried and never soggy. Now, I don't like to mess with perfection, but I secretly think they could up their game by adding squash rings to the menu. Until that day comes, though, I'll have to satisfy my own craving for Fried Squash Rings. The version here is delightful and crunchy, and made with delicata squash. You can certainly use whatever kind of squash your heart desires, but delicata already comes in cylinder form—pretty sweet, right? When you have a hankering for fried food circles, the fewer steps to ring heaven, the better.

YIELDS 15 RINGS

1 (7½-inch [19-cm]) delicata squash, sliced into ½-inch (1.3-cm) thick rings

1 cup (227 ml) buttermilk

3 eggs, whisked

1 tsp hot sauce

1 cup (140 g) medium-grind cornmeal

1 cup (140 g) all-purpose flour

2 tbsp (74 g) herbs de provence

1 tsp ground onion powder

1 tsp ground garlic powder

½ tsp baking powder

¼ tsp kosher salt

¼ tsp ground pepper

Vegetable oil, for frying

In a large bowl, combine the squash rings, buttermilk, eggs and hot sauce. Allow the squash to rest in the buttermilk for at least 30 minutes at room temperature. In another bowl, combine the cornmeal, flour, herbs de provence, onion powder, garlic powder, baking powder, kosher salt and ground pepper.

In a large Dutch oven, pour in vegetable oil, filling to about 2 inches (5 cm) high. Turn the heat to medium-high. Drop a few sprinkles of the cornmeal mixture into the oil and if it starts to sizzle, the oil is hot enough for frying. Using a pair of tongs, grab one of the squash rings, shake off the excess batter and dip it into the cornmeal. Once it is coated, add the squash ring to the oil. I suggest adding about four to five at a time and no more because you don't want to overcrowd the Dutch oven and bring down the heat. Fry the squash rings for about 2 minutes per side or until they are golden brown.

Remove the squash rings from the oil and place them on a plate lined with a paper towel. Garnish with more salt and pepper, if desired. Repeat the process to make the remaining rings, adding more vegetable oil as needed.

Variation: If you can't find delicata squash at the grocery store or famers market, try substituting acorn, carnival or butternut squash.

HALIBUT FILET O' FISH SLIDERS

Growing up Catholic, reeling in a fish dinner on Friday evenings during Lent was a pastime. Unfortunately, I grew up land-locked and seafood options were mostly limited to chain restaurants or frozen fish sticks. These Halibut Filet O' Fish Sliders are my way of making amends for those old-school bland-a-thons, because there's nothing like a fried sandwich made right at home. Fresh halibut fried in a golden batter, topped with tartar sauce and melted cheese and stuffed between two brioche buns. Catch o' the day!

SERVES 4

TARTAR SAUCE

1 cup (232 g) mayonnaise

1 tbsp (4 g) sweet onion relish

1 tbsp (3 g) minced yellow onion

1 tbsp (15 ml) lemon juice

¼ tsp kosher salt

¼ tsp ground pepper

HALIBUT

4 (3-oz [170-g]) halibut filets

2 tbsp (30 ml) lemon juice

1 cup (245 ml) buttermilk

1 tsp kosher salt

1 tsp ground pepper

2 cups (250 g) finely-crushed, unsalted, saltine crackers

½ cup (25 g) panko

1 tbsp (8 g) Old Bay seasoning

Vegetable oil, for frying

4 brioche slider buns

Mild cheddar cheese slices, for garnish

FOR THE TARTAR SAUCE

In a medium bowl, combine the mayonnaise, sweet relish, onion, lemon juice, kosher salt and ground pepper. Set the bowl in the fridge for at least 30 minutes to let the flavors combine.

FOR THE HALIBUT

Place the filets onto a baking sheet and squeeze the lemon juice on top. Next, combine the buttermilk, salt and pepper in a large bowl. In another large bowl, combine the saltine crackers, panko and Old Bay seasoning.

In a large Dutch oven, heat 2 inches (5 cm) of oil until a deep-fry thermometer registers 350°F (177°C). Take a filet and dip it into the buttermilk. Shake off any excess and then dip the filet into the saltine mixture. Place the filet in the oil and fry for 2 minutes. Remove the filet with tongs and place it on a wire rack. Sprinkle it with kosher salt, if desired. Repeat the process with the remaining three fillets.

Meanwhile, preheat the broiler. Place the tops and bottoms of the brioche buns on the baking sheet. Top each of the bottom buns with one slice of cheddar cheese. Place the baking sheet under the broiler until the cheese has slightly melted and the buns are golden and toasty.

To assemble, place a bottom brioche bun on a plate. Top the bun with a halibut filet square and a dollop of the tartar sauce. Add the top of the brioche bun and serve. Repeat the process until all the sandwiches have been assembled!

Variation: If you can't find halibut you can certainly substitute with fresh cod.

CRISPY TURMERIC PARSNIP FRIES

Parsnips get a bum rap. I feel so bad for them—they can't help their cylindrical, white-as-a-ghost exterior. It's a shame. With Sir Russet getting all the French fry attention, grocery shoppers typically walk by the parsnips with their noses held high. Take it from me, though—Crispy Turmeric Parsnip Fries will change your perception of this hearty, winter vegetable. The beauty of these fries is, yes, the simplicity, but the addition of turmeric, paprika and cumin gives the flavor a note of complexity.

SERVES 4

1 lb (450 g) parsnips

5 tbsp (71 g) unsalted butter

1 tsp ground turmeric

1 tsp ground paprika

1 tsp ground cumin

1 tsp kosher salt

1 tsp ground pepper

Peel the parsnips and slice off their tops and bottoms. Cut the parsnips into ¼-inch (6-mm) slices. Bring a large pot of water to a boil and add the parsnips. Cook the parsnips for about 3 minutes, remove, place on a towel to pat dry and after they are dry, place them in a large bowl.

Next, in a large skillet, melt the butter over medium-high heat. Sprinkle the parsnips with turmeric, paprika, cumin, salt and pepper. Toss to make sure the parsnips are well coated. Add the parsnips to the skillet and fry them until they are crispy, or for about 3 to 4 minutes. Remove the parsnips from the skillet and serve them immediately!

Variation: Mix up your vegetable routine by using turnips, cauliflower or rutabagas instead of the parsnips!

Retro Desserts Re-Dished

I'll be honest: My mother is the reason why I bake today. Her patience for sifting flour, rolling out sugar cookie dough and mixing leavening agents taught me that the baking process doesn't have to be mysterious. You just need to work for it (though sometimes I would rather pound dirt than whisk a dozen egg whites by hand to make an angel food cake). My mother taught me to slow down and enjoy the moment, because the real reward of baking isn't the fluffy, lighter-than-air cake—it's the arm workout.

Retro Desserts Re-Dished is full of reimagined traditional desserts that bakers and non-bakers alike can get behind. From Cardamom Carrot Cake with Ginger Marshmallow Frosting (page 174) to Miso Caramel-Apple Slab Pie (page 162) and Cranberry Gingerbread Baked Alaska (page 160), all these desserts honor the past, but they're still sexy enough to serve at a modern dinner table.

CRANBERRY GINGERBREAD BAKED ALASKA

I became a baked Alaska witness at a girls' night hosted by my pal, Jamie. The gang drank giggle juice, ate cheesy pizza and re-watched *Mean Girls* for the hundredth time. At some point, Jamie snuck over to the oven, and like it was no big deal, pulled out a perfectly golden meringue masterpiece and set it on the countertop. Whoa. "Can I be you when I grow up?" I asked. Now, I'm a long way from being a certified home-ec pro, so this Cranberry Gingerbread Baked Alaska is scaled down for good reason. Who has the time or talent to land a three-layer cake? This recipe calls for no-churn gingerbread ice cream, followed by a bourbon-infused cranberry sauce that's layered on top of golden, buttery wafers. All you need to make this dessert is patience and a glass of wine. Unless Jamie happens to be with you. In that case, let her do the baking.

SERVES 4

GINGERBREAD ICE CREAM

1 tsp ground cinnamon

1 tsp ground allspice

1 tsp ground cloves

1 tsp ground ginger

1 tsp ground nutmeg

2 cups (474 ml) heavy whipping cream

1 tbsp (15 ml) vanilla extract

1 (14-oz [400-g]) can sweetened condensed milk

WAFER CRUST

40 vanilla wafers

¼ cup (57 g) unsalted butter, melted

2 tsp (8 g) granulated sugar

CRANBERRY SAUCE

1 cup (100 g) whole fresh cranberries

¼ cup (56 g) granulated sugar

1 tbsp (15 ml) orange juice

1 tbsp (15 ml) bourbon

MERINGUE TOPPING

2 large egg whites

¼ tsp kosher salt

2 tbsp (28 g) granulated sugar

FOR THE GINGERBREAD ICE CREAM

In a small bowl, combine the cinnamon, allspice, cloves, ginger and nutmeg. In a stand mixer fitted with a whisk attachment, add the heavy cream. Begin to whisk the cream on high until stiff peaks form, or about 5 minutes. Reduce the speed of the mixer to low and slowly add the vanilla extract, sweetened condensed milk and the gingerbread spice mixture. Once all of the ingredients are combined, pour the ice cream mixture into a 9 x 5 x 3-inch (23 x 13 x 8-cm) loaf pan. Cover the loaf pan with plastic wrap and freeze for 1 hour.

FOR THE WAFER CRUST

In a food processor, add the vanilla wafers, butter and granulated sugar. Pulse until the crust looks like pea-sized bits. Spray four 7-ounce (207-ml) ramekins with non-stick cooking spray. Take ¼ cup (25 g) of the vanilla wafer mixture and press it into the bottom of each ramekin. Place the ramekins into the freezer for about 10 to 12 minutes to set.

FOR THE CRANBERRY SAUCE

In a medium saucepan, add the whole cranberries and granulated sugar. Turn the heat to medium and stir the cranberries and sugar together. Once the cranberries and sugar start to melt, the cranberries will pop. That's okay! Keep stirring to keep the sugar from burning, or for about 5 minutes. Once the cranberries have softened, remove the saucepan from the heat and let the mixture cool. After the cranberries have cooled, add them to a food processor or blender. Add the orange juice and bourbon. Pulse the cranberries until they are smooth.

Remove the ramekins from the freezer and divide the cranberry sauce among the ramekins, spreading it on top of each crust. Place the ramekins into the freezer for 30 minutes to set.

Remove the prepared ramekins from the freezer and scoop ¼ cup (56 g) of gingerbread ice cream on top of the cranberry layer in each ramekin. Place the ramekins back in the freezer to set for another 30 minutes.

FOR THE MERINGUE TOPPING

Using a hand mixer, beat the egg whites with kosher salt in a large bowl until high peaks form, or for about 4 minutes. Add 2 tablespoons (28 g) of granulated sugar and continue to beat until glossy, or for about 3 minutes. Remove the ramekins from the freezer and top each of them with the whipped meringue, making decorative swirls. Place the ramekins back in the freezer to set for about 2 to 3 hours.

Once set, remove the ramekins from the freezer for the final time and use a kitchen torch or the broiler to brown the meringue tops. Let them rest for 5 minutes and then serve.

*See photo on page 158.

Kitchen Tip: After 1 hour in the freezer, the ice cream will be "soft serve" consistency. Go ahead, scoop it out and place it into each dessert dish. It will completely freeze once it's back in the freezer.

MISO-CARAMEL APPLE SLAB PIE

Apple pie. It's as American as . . . oh, right. If your bucket list is like mine, it includes the item "steal a pie cooling on a windowsill." When I finally pull this off (and I will), I hope the pie is apple. The flavors are as bold and simple as the stars and stripes, and—little known fact—if you eat it with a scoop of vanilla ice cream, you turn into George Washington for half an hour. All kidding aside, I had a blast taking this American classic and giving it an international twist. Miso-Caramel Apple Slab Pie is the result, and it has the added bonus of being super quick to put together. Puff pastry is the foundation, and it's topped with golden apples and a miso-caramel glaze. Better watch your windowsill!

SERVES 4

6 tbsp (85 g) unsalted butter, divided

¾ cup (188 ml) heavy whipping cream

¾ cup (150 g) granulated sugar

2½ tbsp (75 g) light corn syrup

2 tbsp (97 ml) water

¼ cup (165 g) white miso paste

¼ tsp vanilla extract

1 lb (450 g) Granny Smith apples, cored, sliced into ½-inch (1.3-cm) slices

½ tsp ground cinnamon

¼ cup (68 g) brown sugar

¼ tsp kosher salt

1 sheet puff pastry, thawed

1 large egg

Turbinado sugar, for dusting

Vanilla ice cream, for serving

Kitchen Tip: Make the miso caramel a day ahead. Simply reheat it in saucepan and pour it over the golden apples.

Variation: This slab pie also can be made with strawberries or bananas.

Preheat the oven to 400°F (204°C).

In a saucepan preheated to medium heat, melt 3 tablespoons (42 g) of butter. Stir in the cream, making sure it's well combined with the butter. Keep the mixture at medium-low until it is ready to use.

In another large saucepan add the sugar, corn syrup and water. Stir the mixture over medium-high heat until the sugar has dissolved, or for about 4 minutes. Keep stirring until a golden color forms, or for about 5 more minutes. Remove the saucepan from the heat and pour the cream mixture into the saucepan while continuing to whisk. The mixture will start to bubble and that's okay! Keep whisking and the sauce will eventually start to smooth out. Next, add the miso, vanilla extract, and continue to stir until all the ingredients are incorporated and the caramel sauce is smooth. Set it aside until it's ready to add to the pie filling.

In a skillet preheated to medium heat, melt 3 tablespoons (42 g) of the remaining butter. Add the apple slices to the skillet and sauté the apples for about 5 to 6 minutes or until they become lightly golden brown. Turn the heat to medium-low and add the brown sugar, cinnamon and kosher salt to the apples. Stir to combine, making sure the apples are well coated. Keep stirring the apples until they become caramelized, or for about 4 to 5 minutes. Turn off the heat and set the skillet aside.

Cover a baking sheet with parchment paper or a baking mat to prevent sticking. Place the puff pastry on the baking mat. Using a rolling pin, roll the puff pastry sheet into a 10 x 11-inch (25 x 28-cm) rectangle. Next, using a paring knife, cut the pastry dough in half down the center lengthwise so you end up with two pieces. Scoop the apple mixture onto the puff pastry in an equal line down the center leaving a 1-inch (2.54-cm) border. Pour some of the remaining sauce from the skillet on top of the apples along with the miso caramel. It's okay if some of the sauce spills over.

Next, crack an egg into a bowl and whisk. Using a pastry brush, brush the border of the puff pastry lined with apples. Take the second puff pastry sheet and place it directly on top covering the bottom puff pastry sheet and press down on the edges creating a seal. Using a knife, cut roughly five to six slits down the center of the pastry to create a vent. Take the pastry brush and brush the top of the pie with egg wash. Sprinkle the top with turbinado sugar and bake the pie for about 15 to 18 minutes or until golden brown. Remove the pie from the oven and serve it with vanilla ice cream.

BANANA TIRAMISU CAKE TOWERS

My brothers and I ate a lot of banana cake growing up. I think it was my mother's way of secretly making a dessert that was semi-good for us. Aren't moms the best? I still make that famous banana cake of hers from time to time, but I thought hey, why not give this classic cake a shakeup? Banana cake, meet tiramisu; tiramisu, meet banana cake. Let's party! The base of this cake consists mostly of the traditional banana cake. But! I pour brewed coffee over the top to let all those delicious coffee flavors soak into the cake. OH. MY. WORD. Then I assume the tiramisu whipping position—mascarpone, powdered sugar, vanilla extract and cream. Spread this delightful whipped spread over the top, and then dust with cocoa powder. I think my mom is secretly making this dessert right now . . .

YIELDS 3 CAKE TOWERS

½ cup (115 g) unsalted butter, room temperature

1½ cups (300 g) granulated sugar, divided

7 large egg yolks, divided

1⅓ cups (399 g) mashed bananas (approximately 4 small or 2 large)

½ cup (115 g) sour cream

3 tsp (15 ml) vanilla extract, divided

2 cups (280 g) all-purpose flour

1 tsp baking soda

½ tsp kosher salt

½ tsp nutmeg

2 tsp (4 g) espresso powder

4 large egg whites

½ cup (120 ml) strong brewed coffee

1¼ cups (280 g) mascarpone cheese, room temperature

Unsweetened cocoa powder, for dusting

Preheat the oven to 350°F (177°C). Spray a 13 x 9-inch (33 x 23-cm) baking dish with non-stick cooking spray and set it aside. In a stand mixer fitted with a paddle attachment, cream the butter and 1¼ cups (250 g) sugar together. While the mixer is running add 4 egg yolks, one at a time, until combined, followed by the mashed bananas, sour cream and 1 teaspoon of vanilla extract.

In a medium bowl, sift together the flour, baking soda, salt, nutmeg and espresso powder. Next, add the dry ingredients into the wet ingredients while the mixer is running, a third at a time. Once the batter has combined, turn off the mixer.

Using a hand mixer beat the 4 egg whites until they are stiff. Gently fold the egg whites into the batter. Pour the batter into the prepared baking dish. Place the baking dish into the oven and bake it for about 22 to 25 minutes, or until a toothpick inserted into the center comes out clean.

Once the cake is done, remove it from the oven and place it on a wire rack. Pour the coffee on the top of the cake. Let the cake cool completely before frosting and assembling it.

While the cake cools, make the tiramisu frosting. In a stand mixer fitted with a whisk attachment, add 3 egg yolks, ¼ cup (50 g) granulated sugar and 2 teaspoons (10 ml) of vanilla extract. Whisk until smooth and the color is light yellow. Turn off the mixer and then gently fold in the mascarpone cheese.

To assemble the cake, take a 3-inch (8-cm) biscuit cutter and press it into the cake. Cut out six 3-inch (8-cm) circles. Frost all six of the circles with the tiramisu frosting, along with a dusting of cocoa powder. Stack two circles to make one tower. You should have three, two-tiered cake stacks that are ready to be devoured!

Kitchen Tip: Don't have a biscuit cutter handy? Cut out squares instead to make the cake towers!

CHAMPAGNE MARSHMALLOW TREATS

My mother should have received a Nobel prize for whipping up birthday treats at the drop of a hat. Supplying thirty second-graders with trays of marshmallow treats for a certain girl's birthday was no easy task. I don't know how she overcame the pressure. But every year she would save my elementary school reputation with butter, marshmallows and Rice Krispie® cereal mixed together and served in delicious squares. Well, with these Champagne Marshmallow Treats, I'm saving my thirty-something reputation by adding champagne. These marshmallow treats are great for any impromptu party or a certain birthday celebration where a cake just won't do.

YIELDS 10 TREATS

6 tbsp (85 g) unsalted butter

¼ cup (59 ml) dry champagne

6 cups (318 g) mini marshmallows

½ tsp vanilla extract

¼ tsp kosher salt

6 cups (192 g) crisped rice cereal

Line a 9 x 9-inch (23 x 23-cm) baking dish with foil. Spray with non-stick cooking spray and set it aside.

In a large skillet preheated to medium heat, melt the butter. Add the champagne, stir and let it simmer for about minute. Next, add the marshmallows, vanilla extract and kosher salt. Stir the marshmallows until completely melted, or about 4 minutes.

Remove the skillet from the heat and add-in the cereal. Stir to combine. Pour the mixture into the prepared baking dish. Press the mixture into the dish and let it cool completely before slicing it and serving!

Variation: Throw caution to the wind and try these treats with rosé or white wine!

COLORADO PEACH–CRISP POPS

We have a giant peach tree in our front yard. In Denver, Colorado, of all places. When Mr. B and I first moved in, the neighbors all stopped by to say hello and call dibs on a bucket of peaches. Huh? We had no idea what they were talking about. Then in late summer the tree started to bloom, yielding four big buckets of ripe peaches in a single week. Now each summer we give most of our crop away and freeze the rest—which is where these Peach-Crisp Pops come into play. This dessert or snack is easy to assemble and tastes like homemade peach pie. You can use frozen or fresh peaches—just assemble, freeze and enjoy!

YIELDS 8 PEACH-CRISP POPS

6 tbsp (85 g) unsalted butter, divided

2 cups (201 g) oat and honey granola

2 cups (450 g) fresh or frozen (thawed) peach slices, coarsely chopped

½ tsp ground cinnamon

½ tsp vanilla extract

¼ tsp kosher salt

1 tbsp (15 ml) bourbon

1 tbsp (15 ml) water

4 cups (704 g) plain vanilla ice cream, divided

8 (9-oz [250-g]) paper cups

8 popsicle sticks

In a large saucepan over medium heat, melt 2 tablespoons (28 g) of butter. Add the granola and stir until the butter has evenly coated the granola. Toast the granola with the butter for about 2 minutes or until it is lightly golden brown. Turn the heat off and set the saucepan aside.

Meanwhile, in another large skillet preheated to medium-high heat, melt the remaining butter. Add the peach slices to the skillet and cook for a minute or two, stirring to make sure they don't burn. Next, add the cinnamon, vanilla extract, kosher salt, bourbon and water. Stir everything together, making sure all the ingredients are well combined. Continue to sauté the fruit mixture for about 3 to 6 minutes, or until the peaches have softened. Turn off the heat and set the skillet aside to cool completely.

Take a paper cup and place about ¼ cup (44 g) of vanilla ice cream into the bottom. Next, take ¼ cup (35 g) of toasted granola and peaches and place on top of the vanilla ice cream. Top with additional ice cream and press down, making sure the top of the cup has a smooth surface. Push a popsicle stick down into the middle of the cup and place the pop into the freezer. Repeat the process until all the pops have been made. You'll want to freeze the pops for at least 5 hours if not overnight. When you are ready to devour them, remove the pop from the freezer, and, using a pair of scissors, cut away the paper cup.

Variation: Use whatever kind of fruit you have on hand! Apples, bananas, blackberries, blueberries or strawberries would all make an excellent substitution.

BOURBON MATCHA MILKSHAKE

Milkshakes bring all the boys to the yard! (Sorry, couldn't resist.) I say forget Tinder, and whip up a Matcha Bourbon Milkshake for potential crushes instead. While you're shakin' it, you can even drop all sorts of factoid knowledge about matcha: it's a Japanese green tea that's packed with antioxidants and good-mood boosters. Or you can skip the knowledge bomb and get right to the good stuff—smooth vanilla ice cream mixed with matcha brewed tea, milk and bourbon. Pour into a large glass and serve with two straws, and watch the magic happen.

YIELDS 2 MILKSHAKES

2½ cups (190 g) vanilla ice cream

1 cup (240 ml) whole milk

¼ cup (60 ml) bourbon

⅓ cup (80 ml) brewed matcha tea

Matcha powder, for garnish

Whipped cream, for garnish

In a blender or food processor, add the ice cream, milk, bourbon and matcha tea. Pulse until smooth. If it is too thick, add more milk for desired consistency. If it is too thin, add more ice cream. Divide the milkshake between glasses and garnish the tops with matcha powder and whipped cream.

Kitchen Tip: Keep serving glasses in the freezer until you're ready to use them. That way the milkshake stays nice and cold!

PASSION FRUIT–GLAZED PUFF PASTRY DONUTS

When I was a kid, every Sunday after Mass, my brothers and I would bolt to the church gathering space. Behind a stretch of tables, a handful of happy church ladies would always be waiting, with rows of freshly-glazed donuts laid out before them as far as the eye could see. It was our reward for surviving another endless Catholic service. Well, here's my own homage to those hole-y donut memories—Passion Fruit–Glazed Puff Pastry Donuts. Yeah, I guess we're supposed to keep our "passions" in check on Sundays. But passion fruit behaves itself by remaining a bit tart, and when topped with cocoa nibs, you get a righteous flavor that's church-lady approved.

YIELDS 9 DONUTS

3 sheets puff pastry, thawed

Vegetable oil, for frying

1 egg, whisked

1 cup (125 g) powdered sugar

3 tbsp (33 ml) whole milk

1 tsp vanilla extract

2 tbsp (40 g) passion fruit jam

Scant pinch of kosher salt

½ cup (75 g) crushed sweetened cocoa nibs, for garnish

Lightly sprinkle your countertop with flour. Remove the puff pastry sheets from the package and place them on the countertop. Next, take a pastry brush, dip into the whisked egg and brush the top of each puff pastry sheet. Now, take one sheet of puff pastry and place it on top of another. Do this again with the remaining sheet of puff pastry. Once all three sheets are stacked, take a paring knife and cut along the fold seams making three long rectangles. Using a donut cutter, cut out three donuts from each rectangle. Take a sharp knife and cut out a hole in the center of the donut. You should end up with around nine donuts.

Next, add the vegetable oil to a large Dutch oven, filling it to about 3 to 4 inches (8 to 10 cm) high. Using a fry thermometer, preheat the oil to 350°F (177°C). Fry each donut for about 2 to 3 minutes or until it is golden brown. Place the donut on a wire rack and repeat the process until all the donuts have been fried.

To make the passion fruit glaze, whisk together the powdered sugar, milk, vanilla extract, passion fruit jam and a pinch of kosher salt. Take a donut and dip the top of it into the glaze. Garnish with crushed cocoa nibs. Repeat the process until all of the donuts have been glazed!

Kitchen Tip: Have leftover puff pastry? Fry up the extra scraps and use them as a topping on other desserts or simply snack on them!

Variation: If you can't find passion fruit at the grocery store, try using mango or pineapple puree.

CARDAMOM-SPICED CARROT CAKE
with GINGER MARSHMALLOW FROSTING

Carrot cake and I haven't always seen eye-to-eye. My loyalty when it comes to indulging in sweets lies with chocolate. Predictable, yes. But nothing goes better with a glass of red vino than a few handfuls of frozen dark chocolate chips. It wasn't until a Denver Friendsgiving when my friend, Megan, who is a fabulous baker, brought a three-tiered carrot cake for dessert that my eyes began to wander. This carrot cake was a thing of beauty. Perfectly fluffy and covered in a cream cheese frosting that would make you swoon with the single lick of a finger. Megan's cake showed me that chocolate doesn't always reign supreme, and this Cardamom-Spiced Carrot Cake with Ginger Marshmallow Frosting proves it, too. Cardamom gives this moist cake a little somethin', somethin'. A little shimmy, if you will. With the addition of my favorite ginger marshmallow frosting, this cake will turn any chocolate snob into a carrot cake believer.

SERVES 6 TO 8

CARDAMOM-SPICED CARROT CAKE

2 cups (250 g) all-purpose flour

2 tsp (14 g) baking soda

¼ tsp kosher salt

2 tsp (4 g) ground cardamom

2 tsp (4 g) ground cinnamon

¼ tsp ground nutmeg

¼ tsp ground cloves

3 large eggs

¾ cup (185 ml) buttermilk

¾ cup (185 ml) vegetable oil

1¼ cups (250 g) granulated sugar

1 tsp vanilla extract

2 cups (100 g) shredded carrots

1 cup (125 g) chopped walnuts

1 cup (150 g) golden raisins

GINGER MARSHMALLOW FROSTING

2 large egg whites

¼ tsp kosher salt

¼ cup (50 g) granulated sugar

¾ cup (185 g) corn syrup

1 tsp vanilla extract

1 tbsp (6 g) grated fresh ginger

FOR THE CARDAMOM-SPICED CARROT CAKE

Preheat the oven to 350°F (177°C). Lightly grease and flour two 8-inch (20-cm) round cake pans and set them aside. In a large bowl, sift together the flour, baking soda, kosher salt, cardamom, cinnamon, nutmeg and cloves. In another large mixing bowl, add the eggs and whisk them until they are combined. Next, add the buttermilk, oil, sugar and vanilla extract. Whisk until all the ingredients are well incorporated.

Take the wet ingredients and add them to the dry ingredients in thirds. This way the batter has time to absorb wet-to-dry. In a medium bowl, combine the carrots, walnuts and raisins. Gently fold the carrot mixture into the batter until all ingredients are well combined. Pour the batter into the prepared cake pans. Bake the cakes for about 1 hour, or until a toothpick inserted into the middle of the cake comes out clean.

Once baked, remove the cakes from the oven and set them aside to cool completely before removing them from the pan.

FOR THE GINGER MARSHMALLOW FROSTING

In a stand mixer fitted with a whisk attachment, beat the egg whites with salt until frothy. Gradually add the sugar, beating until soft peaks form. Pour the corn syrup into a microwaveable glass dish. Heat the syrup in the microwave until it boils, or about 60 seconds. Once the syrup is boiling, remove it from the microwave and pour it in a thin stream over the egg white mixture, a little at a time. Continue beating on high speed until stiffer peaks form. Add in the vanilla and fresh ginger, and beat until glossy.

Once the cakes have cooled completely, remove the cake pans and set the first layer on a cake stand. Using a spatula, spread some of the ginger marshmallow frosting on top of the layer. Next, place the second layer top-side down. Cover the cake with more frosting. Serve and enjoy!

BANANAS FOSTER GALETTE

I don't call myself a baker. It requires a little too much science, and a little too much patience. I leave the baking mitts to my sister-in-law, Kelly, who's a wizard when it comes to working with flour and dough. Do your thing, girl! But we non-bakers still need dessert, right? Enter bananas foster. Now, when I hear someone say bananas foster, I think New Orleans circa 1953—this classic American dessert was created at the world-famous Brennan's on Bourbon Street, after all. Ripe bananas are seared in a hot skillet, then covered in brown sugar, cinnamon, vanilla and rum! This version is what I call meeting the baking world halfway. Make the bananas foster, let it cool, add it to pie dough and then back off. It's non-baker and baker approved!

SERVES 4

2 tbsp (28 g) unsalted butter

2 large bananas, cut on the bias (about 18 slices)

1 cup (200 g) light brown sugar

1 tsp vanilla extract

½ tsp ground cinnamon

¼ tsp kosher salt

1 tbsp (15 ml) rum

2 tbsp (18 g) all-purpose flour

1 package store-bought pie dough, thawed

3 tbsp (45 ml) milk

1 tbsp (12 g) granulated sugar

Ice cream, for garnish

Preheat the oven to 375°F (191°C).

In a medium skillet preheated to medium-high heat, melt the butter. Next add the banana slices and let them cook for about 1 minute per side. Then add the brown sugar, vanilla extract, cinnamon and kosher salt and cook for about 2 minutes. Lower the heat to medium and continue to stir gently. It's okay if the bananas start to break apart or look like mush. They will still be fantastic! Next, add the rum. Caution! It may flame, and that's okay. Quickly remove the skillet from the heat and turn off the stove. Cool the bananas foster.

Dust your countertop with all-purpose flour. Place the pie dough on top of the counter and roll it out into a circle that is about 11 inches (28 cm) in diameter. Carefully transfer the pie dough to a baking sheet lined with parchment paper. Next, take the bananas foster filling and place the filling in the middle of the pie dough. It's okay if some of the mixture starts to escape because this pie is rustic! Fold over the edge of the dough to create a 2-inch (5-cm) border around the galette. Take a pastry brush and brush the milk all along the border, followed by the sugar. Bake the galette for about 20 to 25 minutes or until the pie dough turns golden brown. Remove it from the oven and let it rest for 10 minutes. Transfer the galette to a cutting board and serve it with ice cream.

Kitchen Tip: You can certainly make this version without using alcohol. Simply add 1 teaspoon of rum extract to the skillet instead of the rum.

PISTACHIO & MINT DARK CHOCOLATE CUPS

My go-to, never-fail, can-always-count-on to satisfy my sweet tooth is a handful of frozen dark chocolate chips, right out of the bag. Call it simple, but there's something about the crunch and flavor of seventy percent dark chocolate that instantly makes me giddy. I've come a long way from chocolate peanut butter cups, that's for sure, but there's a very happy medium—these Pistachio and Mint Dark Chocolate Cups. Move over Willy Wonka, because these decadent treats aren't goofing around. These cups are dangerously easy to make and are filled with crushed pistachio, fresh mint and coconut flakes. Make a big batch and keep them in the freezer to nibble on. They'll satisfy any sweet tooth and make your inner seven-year-old giddy, too!

YIELDS 12 CHOCOLATE CUPS

3 cups (462 g) dark chocolate chips, divided

1½ cups (198 g) shelled pistachios

¾ cup (24 g) fresh chopped mint

6 tbsp (84 g) unsweetened coconut flakes

3 tbsp (45 ml) agave or honey

6 tbsp (90 ml) coconut milk

Line a 12-cup muffin pan with muffin liners and set it aside.

Bring a medium saucepan filled with about 2 to 3 inches (5 to 8 cm) of water to a boil. In a medium mixing bowl, add 2 cups (350 g) of dark chocolate chips. Set the bowl over the saucepan, making sure the bottom is not touching the water, and stir the chocolate until it is melted and smooth, about 1 minute. Next, take 1 tablespoon (15 ml) of the melted chocolate and place it into the bottom of each muffin liner. Using a pastry brush, brush some of the chocolate up the sides of the liner about three-quarters of the way. It will look thin, but once the chocolate sets it will look just right. Once all the liners have been filled, place the muffin pan into the fridge to set for about 30 to 40 minutes.

In a food processor add the pistachios, mint, coconut flakes, agave and coconut milk. Pulse to combine until the pistachios are finely chopped and everything has come together. Take the muffin pan out of the fridge and place it on the countertop. Next, take a tablespoon (15 ml) of the pistachio-mint mixture and place it into the center of each chocolate cup. Press down on the mixture, making sure it's flat. Place the muffin pan back into the fridge for another 5 to 10 minutes.

While the mixture sets, melt the remaining 1 cup (154 g) of dark chocolate chips. Once it's melted, remove the bowl from the saucepan and set it aside. Next, remove the muffin pan from the fridge. Spoon a tablespoon (15 ml) of the melted chocolate over the pistachio-mint mixture. Repeat this process until all the cups have been covered. Place the muffin pan into the fridge again and let the chocolate set, for about 15 minutes.

Once the chocolate is set, remove the muffin pan from the fridge. Remove the muffin liner from the chocolate cup and enjoy!!

Kitchen Tip: Your refrigerator too full to fit a muffin tin? Line individual oven-safe six-ounce custard cups with the muffin liners to save some real estate while the chocolate sets!

POMEGRANATE KOMBUCHA FLOATS

Jimmy's Diner, it was called. When you stepped into Jimmy's, it was like stepping back into the 1950s: mid-century Americana complete with red booths, a jukebox with classic Elvis tunes and vinyl records lining the walls. A cheeseburger, fries and a float was a must-order. So, here's to Jimmy's, and the classic American diner—and, here's to updates! The kombucha used in this float is a fermented tea with natural probiotics—a great, healthier alternative to soda. Just add ice cream to a glass, top it with pomegranate seeds and juice, then pour kombucha into the glass till it's filled to the rim. Serve with a straw and enjoy!

YIELDS 2 FLOATS

8 scoops (904 g) vanilla ice cream

2 tbsp (20 g) pomegranate seeds

½ cup (119 ml) pomegranate juice

1 pint (473 ml) pomegranate kombucha

In the bottom of an 8-ounce (236-ml) drinking glass, place 1 scoop of ice cream. Sprinkle 1 teaspoon of pomegranate seeds on top followed by 1 tablespoon (15 ml) of the pomegranate juice. Repeat these steps 3 more times. Next, fill the glass with pomegranate kombucha. It's okay if it overflows! Repeat the process with the remaining glasses. Serve with a straw and enjoy.

Kitchen Tip: After you've filled the glass with ice cream, pomegranate seeds and pomegranate juice, freeze the glass before pouring in the kombucha. It will help keep the float more intact.

Variation: Don't have pomegranate kombucha handy? Any flavor of kombucha will be a great substitute! Try using lemon-ginger kombucha and garnish with crystallized ginger for a fun twist!

Tips and Tricks for Modern Comfort Cooking

Making comfort food modern doesn't have to be frustrating. I promise. In this section, I provide you with a few tips and tricks that will make success yours.

Unlike our mothers, we live in a time where we have access to more than just salmon in a can, fruit cocktail and jello salads. Now, things like international spices, super foods, gluten-free grains, probiotic drinks, veggie noodles and nut butters are making life interesting. If ever there was a time to learn to cook, it is now!

A few things come to mind for creating tasty and unique comfort food: clarified butter, homemade pickled foods and spiral-shaped vegetables. All three can help you master modern comfort food.

HOW TO MAKE CLARIFIED BUTTER

Butter is your friend and will make anything taste like a million dollars. But why clarified butter? Let me explain first that butter is eighty percent fat and fifteen percent water with a few additional milk proteins mixed in. Plain ol' butter has a very low smoke point, which can cause problems when you need to make a sauce or to sauté veggies. Clarified butter does not contain milk proteins or water. It is pure butterfat with a smoke point of 450°F (232°C).

I use clarified butter in recipes that require HEAT. High heat gives meats a yummy caramelized flavor, and also cooks veggies quickly for a crisp, delicious result.

Clarified butter is super simple to make. Simply heat a medium-size saucepan until it is medium-hot. Add two sticks of unsalted butter and let them melt. Once the butter melts, remove the saucepan from the heat.

The foamy milk proteins in the melted butter will have floated to the top. Take a spoon and skim the foam off the top leaving the butterfat in the saucepan. Once you've removed the foam, pour the clarified butter into a container. Make sure it's completely cool before storing with a tight-fitting lid. Clarified butter can be kept in the fridge for up to three months! Are we buttah friends now?

HOW TO MAKE SPIRAL-SHAPED VEGETABLES

Do you know what a zoodle is? It is a "noodle" made from a vegetable, cut into a spiral shape. If you love pasta, but don't want to feel like you are wearing a carb load for the next three days, vegetable noodles are here to save the day!

You can "spiralize" just about any vegetable you see at the grocery store or farmer's market. Zucchini is the most popular, but butternut squash, carrots, parsnips, onions or bell peppers can also be used. A few of the recipes in this cookbook are made using vegetable noodles. Some of these recipes are: Shrimp Scampi and Zucchini Noodle Bake (page 113), Chicken Puttanesca Sweet Potato Noodle Skillet (page 139) and Chicken and Andouille with Carrot Noodles (page 131).

One of the most fun aspects of spiralizing, besides the health benefit, is that you get to play with your food. Subbing different vegetables in your favorite comfort foods is like winning the food lottery! If you want to lighten up a recipe in this book, or a favorite of your own, go for it!

SPIRALIZED NOODLES

You can make them in one of two ways. You can purchase a spiralizer that does the work for you. I have one at home and I love, love, using it! Or, you can use a vegetable or julienne peeler you have at home. Just peel the vegetable all the way down to create the kind of vegetable ribbons you desire. Just make sure you peel the skin off vegetables with a thick or tough skin like sweet potatos or carrots. This will create a smoother and more consistent noodle. You can also eat vegetable noodles raw, in a salad or add them to a broth and make a soup!

HOW TO MAKE QUICK PICKLES

Forget spending hours in front of a hot tub full of canning jars, because quick pickling is where the squad is hanging out! The goal of quick pickling is to add a burst of freshness and crunch to any meal.

You can pickle almost any vegetable. For this cookbook, I've narrowed it down to four essential quick-pickling recipes which you'll find over the next several pages—dill pickles, bread and butter pickles, carrots and onions. Each recipe is easy and full of flavor!

QUICK DILL PICKLES

We start with the mighty dill pickle—our burgers and sandwiches bow to thee! The best news? This recipe only uses a few ingredients, so you can make as many or as few pickles as you want.

2 PINTS (946 ML)

EQUIPMENT
2 small-mouth, pint-size (473-ml) glass Mason jars or 1 wide-mouth Mason jar, with lids and rings

Tongs

BRINE
1 cup (240 ml) water

¾ cup (180 ml) apple cider vinegar

2 tsp (12 g) kosher salt

1 tsp granulated sugar

DILL PICKLES
3 to 4 cloves garlic

6 baby cucumbers

6 fresh dill sprigs

½ tsp red pepper flakes (1 tsp if you like things hot)

Wash the Mason jars, lids and rings in hot soapy water or sterilize them in the dishwasher. Pour the water and apple-cider vinegar into a metal saucepan. Add the kosher salt and the sugar. Stir to combine. Bring the mixture to a boil, approximately 10 minutes. When the brine has come to a full boil for 1 minute, turn off the heat and let the mixture cool a minute.

Meanwhile, chop the garlic into small pieces and place them into a small bowl. Cut off the ends of the baby cucumbers and slice the cucumbers in half. Slice the halves lengthwise so that you have two to three cucumber spears per cucumber half. Slice at least five to six cucumbers and put the spears into a small bowl. Next, roughly chop the dill sprigs and place them into another small bowl.

Place a few spears (about 4 or 5) into the bottom of the glass pint jar. Sprinkle in a few pieces of garlic. Add 2 to 3 sprigs of dill. Sprinkle a bit of the red pepper over the vegetables. Repeat the same process as above, layering a few cucumber spears into the jar, and then sprinkling garlic and dill and red pepper over and around them.

Now take a ¼-cup (60-ml) measuring cup and fill it with warm brine. Pour the brine over the layered cucumbers. TAP the jar to let the contents settle, then pour more brine over the vegetables until the brine just covers the vegetables. Tap the jar again on the counter to remove any air bubbles. Make sure you leave ½ inch (1.3 cm) of headspace at the top to allow the pickles to expand in the jar. Headspace is the amount of space in a jar needed to allow for expansion of liquid or contents while settling. Put the lid and ring on the jar and screw until firm.

Here's the difficult part: Put the pickles into the refrigerator. Let them sit and rest for at least FOUR days! The cucumbers and brine need to "marry" their flavors and cure. The pickles will be ready to eat after four days, and they last, stored in the refrigerator, for up to one month.

QUICK BREAD & BUTTER PICKLES

These pickles are perfect on sandwiches, on top of chili or when you need a little crunchy snack! Make sure to get the freshest cucumbers possible. This recipe can be easily doubled which means more pickles for all!

4 PINTS (1.9 L)

EQUIPMENT
4 small-mouth, pint-size (473-ml) glass Mason jars, with lids and rings

Tongs

BREAD AND BUTTER PICKLES
1½ lb (680 g) smaller, pickling cucumbers

1 cup (150 g) finely chopped yellow onion

1½ tbsp (27 g) kosher salt

½ cup (120 ml) water

1¼ cups (275 g) brown sugar

1½ cups (360 ml) apple cider vinegar

½ tsp celery seed

½ tsp ground tumeric

2 tsp (8 g) yellow mustard seed

¼ tsp ground cloves or allspice

Wash the jars, the rings and lids in hot soapy water or sanitize in the dishwasher. Set the jars aside until they are ready to fill.

Next, prep the vegetables by washing and scrubbing the skins of the cucumbers. Trim off the cucumber ends and slice the cucumbers into slices about ¼-inch (6-mm) thick. Peel the onion and cut it in half lengthwise, from pole-to-pole. Then cut each half cross-wise into ¼-inch (6-mm) slices.

In a non-reactive glass or plastic bowl, place the cucumbers and onions. Toss with the kosher salt, using your hands to lightly toss the vegetables and get the salt dispersed throughout. Cover the bowl and put it into the refrigerator for 1 to 2 hours. Take out the vegetables and put them into a colander. Rinse them well with water and let them drain. Toss the vegetables around a bit in the colander to shift their positions, then rinse them again with water. Let them drain well again.

Next, you'll make the brine! Combine the water, brown sugar, apple cider vinegar, celery seed, turmeric, yellow mustard seed and ground cloves in a medium saucepan. Bring the mixture to a boil over high heat and stir to dissolve the sugar. Reduce the heat to low, and simmer for 3 minutes. Remove the brine from the heat and let it cool slightly.

Using a pair of tongs, pack the cucumbers and onions into pint-size Mason jars. Pour the brine over the vegetables until they are covered. Tap the jar on the counter to settle the ingredients and remove the air bubbles. Put the lids and rings on the jars and store them in the refrigerator for at least 24 hours before eating. The pickles keep in the fridge up to one month.

EASY PICKLED CARROTS

Forget reaching for baby carrots to snack on. These easy pickled carrots are the new go-to when it comes to modern snacking. Enjoy as a single carrot or add to a charcuterie board to kick things up a notch!

2 PINTS (946 ML)

EQUIPMENT

2 small-mouth, pint-size (473-ml) glass Mason jars, with lids and rings

Tongs

CARROTS

3 to 4 medium carrots

1 cup (240 ml) water

1 cup (240 ml) distilled white vinegar

3 tbsp (45 g) granulated sugar

½ tsp kosher salt

2 tsp (8 g) pickling spices (see kitchen tip)

Wash the jars and rings and lids in hot, soapy water, or sterilize them in the dishwasher. Set them aside until they are ready to fill.

Next, peel the skins from the carrots and trim off the ends. Cut each carrot in half, or thirds, if the carrot is super long! Then cut each of the halves into ½-inch (1.3-cm) sticks. Put all of the carrot sticks into a bowl.

Time to make the brine! Put the water, vinegar, sugar, kosher salt and pickling spices into a medium-size saucepan. Stir to combine. Bring the mixture to a boil over medium-high heat. Let the mixture boil for one minute, then turn off the heat. Stir again to make sure the sugar is dissolved. Let the brine cool before assembling the jars.

Once the brine has cooled, divide the carrot sticks evenly between the two pint-size Mason jars. Pour the brine over the pickles leaving ½-inch (1.3-cm) headspace from the brine to the edge of the jar. Tap the jar on the countertop to settle the contents and release any air bubbles.

Screw on the lids and rings. Store the pickled carrots in the refrigerator. You can eat the carrots within 24 hours. They keep in the refrigerator for 2 to 3 weeks.

> *Kitchen Tip:* Pickling spices are a common combination of spices often used in pickling and also to marinate brisket. You can purchase a bottle for around two dollars and it keeps up to one year. A pickling spice mixture usually contains bay leaves, mustard seeds, celery seeds, whole peppercorns, allspice berries, whole cloves, cinnamon, coriander and others, depending on the brand. You can also make your own if you want, but it is typically cheaper to purchase them pre-made.

EASY PICKLED ONIONS

Making pickled onions is not only delicious, but there is zero hassle! You slice, stir, pour and pack. That's it! You will be adding these crunchy garnishes to every taco, burger or salad.

2 PINTS (946 ML)

EQUIPMENT

2 small-mouth, pint-size (473-ml) glass Mason jars, with lids and rings

Tongs

ONIONS

1 large red onion

1 cup (240 ml) water

½ cup (120 ml) distilled white vinegar

1 tbsp (15 g) granulated sugar

1½ tsp (9 g) kosher salt

1 tsp pickling spices

Wash the Mason jars, along with the lids and rings, in hot soapy water or sterilize the jars in the dishwasher. Set them aside until they ready to fill.

Next, cut off the ends of the onion, and peel off the skin. Cut the onion in half, length-wise. Cut in halves again, making four quarters. Finally, slice each quarter into ½-inch (1.3-cm) strips of onion and put all the onion strips into a bowl.

Assemble the brine! In a small bowl, stir together the water, vinegar, sugar, kosher salt and pickling spice. Make sure to whisk everything together until the sugar and salt are dissolved. Next, pack the onion slices into the jars. Pour the brine over the onions and tap the jar on the countertop to settle the contents. Make sure there is ½-inch (1.3-cm) headspace from the jar top to allow room for the contents to expand. Screw the lid and ring onto the jar and put it in the refrigerator for at least 2 hours to overnight for better results. Pickled onions last in the refrigerator for 2 to 3 weeks.

Acknowledgments

This cookbook would not have come to fruition without the help of some extraordinary people. Mr. B, your love and endless encouragement throughout the writing of this book is something for which I will always be thankful. Mom and Dad, your constant reassurance to trust my gut and never give up helped me to believe that, in the end, good things will come. Aunt Joan, without your culinary brilliance, this book would not be possible. Thank you, from the bottom of my heart, for taking time from your life to be my extra set of eyes and hands. You were a voice of reason and a saving grace when it came to making these recipes come to life. This book is half yours. Uncle Bruce, you're the best taste-tester a girl could ever have. Truly, your palate is wise. John and Sarah, without you two this book would be a rambling mess. Thank you for being an honest sounding board. Grier family, if not for y'all, Climbing Grier Mountain would not be possible. Thank you for being constant advocates throughout my blogging career. This cookbook is a true testament to your love and encouragement. Denver Village, without your support and comic relief I'm not sure I would have survived. Thank you for being the best cheerleaders, and believing in my foodie dreams. To my loyal readers of Climbing Grier Mountain—I bow to you in gratitude. You are the reason this book is here. Thank you for reading about my shenanigans day-in and day-out, and for your relentless loyalty. To the amazing team at Page Street Publishing who worked tirelessly behind the scenes and for giving a girl a chance to fulfill a dream. And thanks to Jean Sagendorph, my agent—you fought every day to make this cookbook come to life. Your dedication to this book is the reason I get to share my love for cooking. I owe you a meal . . . or two.

About the Author

Lauren Grier is the writer and photographer behind Climbing Grier Mountain, a food and travel blog. Her recipes and writing have been featured in nationally recognized publications and websites, including *Food Network*, *Bon Appétit*, *BuzzFeed* and *The Huffington Post*. She has worked with well-known domestic and international tourism boards, including Scotland, Yountville, California and Germany.

Lauren is a down-to-earth authority on turning every day, ho-hum meals, cocktails and desserts into fresh and flavorful crowd-favorites through a twist of adventure. If you can't find her in the kitchen, she is probably taking pictures, exercising her creative or actual muscles, or hosting a get-together for "the Village"—otherwise known as her dearest friends. She also loves to unearth distinct aspects of Denver, where she calls home.

Index